Mathematical Applications in
Political Science
VI

Mathematical Applications in Political Science VI

Edited by James F. Herndon and Joseph L. Bernd
Virginia Polytechnic Institute
and State University

The University Press of Virginia

Charlottesville

THE UNIVERSITY PRESS OF VIRGINIA
Copyright © 1972 by the Rector and Visitors
of the University of Virginia

First published 1972

ISBN: 0-8139-0386-6
Library of Congress Catalog Card Number: 67–28023
Printed in the United States of America

Contents

Tables

Figures

Mathematical Applications in
Political Science
VI

Introduction

James F. Herndon and Joseph L. Bernd
Virginia Polytechnic Institute and
State University

IF THIS volume had appeared thirty years ago, it would probably have contained papers employing statistical techniques for data analysis and hypothesis testing. Quantitative work in political science still relies heavily and with much profit on statistical methods. But political scientists have long since begun to use mathematical structures not only to manipulate data but to construct simplified models of the political process.

By identifying key parameters of the process in which he is interested and by expressing these in mathematical language, the investigator is able to use mathematics as a construct. In turn, he is able to manipulate the language of the construct rather than the elements of the process. The result of these efforts, if successful, is an understanding of the process as it may occur in different states or under assumptions about its elements that differ from those required when studying the process "in nature."

Not infrequently, the construction of a mathematical model may lead to the discovery that conventional views of the process under study are not wrong but incomplete. That discovery may follow from study of a model that bears a remarkable closeness of fit to one set of data but not to another. The first paper in this volume,[1] Fred Kort's "Linear and Nonlinear Functions as Criteria for Distinction between Judicial Decisions

---

[1] These papers were presented to participants in the 1970 summer Institute in Mathematical Applications in Political Science conducted at Virginia Polytechnic Institute and State University and supported by the National Science Foundation. Other volumes in the series are: John M. Claunch (ed.), *Mathematical Applications in Political Science* (Dallas: Arnold Foundation of Southern Methodist University, 1965); Joseph L. Bernd (ed.), *Mathematical Applications in Political Science, II* (Dallas: Southern Methodist University Press, 1966); Joseph L. Bernd (ed.), *Mathematical Applications in Political Science, III* (Charlottesville: University Press of Virginia, 1967); Joseph L. Bernd (ed.), *Mathematical Applications in Political Science, IV* (Charlottesville: University Press of Virginia, 1969); and James F. Herndon and Joseph L. Bernd (eds.), *Mathematical Applications in Political Science, V* (Charlottesville: University Press of Virginia, 1971).

in Different Legal Systems," is an example of one such use of mathematical modeling.

Kort finds support in his work for the notion that Common Law and Civil Law courts are distinguished by the degree of their reliance on statutory provisions. But Kort also discovers that the decisive difference in these court systems is the requirement in Civil Law jurisdictions of certain indispensable conditions. The Common Law court he examines, on the other hand, works within a more tentative framework which sets no such indispensable conditions. Kort is led to his conclusions after discovering that while the decision data in the Common Law court can be accounted for by a linear model, the same model cannot be applied to the decisions of the Civil Law court. The latter court's decisions are shown to fit a nonlinear model, which Kort is able to define substantively as one that requires particular conditions to be met in fact situations before decisions favorable to a petitioner can be made.

One of the most influential models in political science to have been constructed in the last decade is that which informs William H. Riker's work in political coalitions.[2] The remaining three papers in this collection stem from Riker's work and illustrate additional investigative properties of mathematical models.

"A General Theory of the Calculus of Voting," by Richard D. McKelvey and Peter C. Ordeshook, makes more general (and adds a qualification to) earlier work by Ordeshook and Riker [3] and offers important insights into the electoral process. The authors develop a model which challenges the view that voting ought to be thought of as an irrational act. Taking into account the expected utility of voting less the expected utility of abstention under varying degrees of competition, they suggest two implications of the model that turn out to be anything but obvious. These implications also run counter to some generally held notions concerning the efficacy of voting. The authors find, first, that the addition of a third candidate (to a two-candidate election) may decrease the efficacy of voting for some voters and, secondly, that the efficacy of voting for some voters may increase as one candidate is thought or known to be ahead of his two opponents. These propositions now await the development and application of some appropriate empirical test.

Steven J. Brams's and William H. Riker's "Models of Coalition Formation in Voting Bodies" derives more directly from Riker's theory of political coalitions. Following a discussion of coalition formation proc-

[2] William H. Riker, *The Theory of Political Coalitions* (New Haven: Yale University Press, 1962).

[3] William H. Riker and Peter C. Ordeshook, "A Theory of the Calculus of Voting," *American Political Science Review*, LXII (March, 1968), 25–42.

esses (and the arguments favoring pertinent assumptions), Brams and Riker are able to construct several mathematically distinct models that represent such processes. Examination of the models and their implications leads to identification of those points in the process of coalition formation at which a coalition can be expected to win (or lose) and of the costs and benefits to members who join a coalition at various points in the process of its formation. Appropriate hypotheses are taken from the model and applied to data on four national nominating conventions. The model and the evidence suggest a mathematical uniformity (under specified conditions) in trends that underlie bandwagon effects in a national convention. It seems, for example, that once a candidate attains about 42 per cent of the convention's votes, he is very likely never to be headed by his competitors. The convention data also lead the authors to suggest modifications in the model as well as in less rigorous interpretations of convention dynamics.

The final work in the collection, William H. Riker's "Three-Person Coalitions in Three-Person Games: Experimental Verification of the Theory of Games," reports an effort to compare laboratory data with a model of coalition formation. The setting is one in which three persons enter into pairwise negotiations over the division of dollar amounts the investigator supplies. Predicted results occur, but so does the unexpected. What was mathematically possible in the model but assumed not to be behaviorally significant did take place in a series of trials. Because the model allows for such unanticipated results, the unexpected is rendered explicable, and one's confidence in the generality of the model is increased.

The substantive concerns in these papers center on processes taking place in judicial, nominating convention, electoral, and laboratory contexts. The models the authors develop fit these situations, but if there is something we may properly call political, the models ought to be capable of extension to other and superficially quite different contexts. We hope that the publication of these papers will encourage other scholars to make these extensions, where needed to modify the models presented here, and to create models of their own.

Steven J. Brams is Associate Professor in the Department of Politics, Graduate School of Arts and Sciences, New York University. He received his doctorate at Northwestern University. Fred Kort is Professor of Political Science, Department of Political Science, University of Connecticut. He also holds a doctorate from Northwestern University. Richard D. McKelvey is Assistant Professor of Political Science in the Department of Political Science at the University of Rochester, where he received his doctorate. Peter C. Ordeshook is Associate Professor of Political Science, School of Urban and Public Affairs, Carnegie-Mellon University. His doctorate was also conferred by the University of Rochester. William H. Riker is Professor and Chairman of the Department of Political Science at the University of Rochester. He received his doctorate at Harvard University.

Linear and Nonlinear Functions as Criteria for Distinction between Judicial Decisions in Different Legal Systems

1 Fred Kort
University of Connecticut

COMPARATIVE studies of legal systems have devoted considerable attention to Civil Law systems and Common Law systems—legal systems which characterize the administration of justice in many different societies. The traditional distinction between these respective legal systems in terms of primary reliance on statutory sources in the former (influenced by the reception of the Roman law) and emphasis on judicial precedent in the latter has been subject to modification in recent decades.[1] It has been suggested that a more decisive consideration for a comparison of these two categories of legal systems would be the following difference: In Civil Law jurisdictions, a formal conceptual structure is developed prior to the application of legal principles to judicial decisions. In Common Law systems, on the other hand, a merely tentative conceptual framework is accepted, with the expectation that it will assume more concrete forms in the process of judicial experience.[2] On the basis of this general statement, it is not apparent how the indicated difference manifests itself in adjudication in the respective legal systems. What constitutes formal structure or merely a tentative framework in legal concepts may—without further qualifications—depend on intuitive judgment and be the subject of varying opinions. It is the purpose of this study to show that, in at least one area of adjudication in a Common Law system and a Civil system, the suggested conceptual difference can be stated in an unambiguous form by employing linear and nonlinear functions.

Support for the earlier phases of this research was provided by a grant awarded by the Division of Social Sciences of the National Science Foundation. The IBM 360 System at the Computer Center of the University of Connecticut, supported by National Science Foundation grant no. GJ-9, was used extensively throughout this research. The assistance that has been received from the National Science Foundation and from the University is gratefully acknowledged.

[1] See, e.g., F. H. Lawson, *A Common Lawyer Looks at the Civil Law* (Ann Arbor, Mich.: University of Michigan Law School, 1953), especially pp. 45–90.

[2] *Ibid.*, pp. 66–69.

The area of adjudication that has been selected for the purpose of this comparative study is the field of workmen's compensation cases. One reason for this choice is the availability of a sufficient number of cases in the respective jurisdictions for adequate samples. This would not be true, for example, in the field of constitutional law. Another reason is that workmen's compensation is a part of administrative law, where some convergence between Civil Law systems and Common Law systems can be noted, in spite of the fact that in the former a special administrative court reviews cases even on the highest appellate level (at least this applies to the example that will be examined), whereas in the latter ordinary courts perform this function. If, therefore, differences in adjudication in this area of law can be detected, it would be reasonable to expect that in more divergent areas of law these differences in adjudication in Civil Law and Common Law systems would be even more pronounced.

As an example from a Common Law system, the Connecticut workmen's compensation cases were chosen, on which an earlier study had been prepared.[3] They are representative of American workmen's compensation cases in several respects.[4] As in more than four-fifths of the states, disputes in Connecticut workmen's compensation cases are originally adjudicated by administrative agencies, where the Common Law rules of assumption of risk, contributory negligence, and the fellow-servant relationship are not applicable. The decisions of the workmen's compensation commissioners may be appealed to the Superior Court and are subject to further review by the State Supreme Court. As in approximately three-fifths of the states, employers in Connecticut are insured exclusively through private companies, and the statutory provisions do not specify occupational diseases but leave such determinations to the courts.

As a corresponding example from a Civil Law system, the Swiss workmen's compensation cases were selected. The reason for this choice was that Switzerland is one of the very few states of continental Europe with a legal system that has not been affected by political changes related to World War I and World War II. As a result, it has been possible to analyze cases covering a period of several decades of the twentieth century—corresponding to the same period in the American states—without the interference of the variable that would be introduced by basic changes in the legal system. It is noteworthy in this connection

---

[3] See Fred Kort, "A Nonlinear Model for the Analysis of Judicial Decisions," *American Political Science Review*, LXII (June, 1968), 546–55.

[4] For a comparison of the administration of workmen's compensation in the various states, see Arthur Larson, *The Laws of Workmen's Compensation* (New York: Matthew Bender, 1967 –).

that the Connecticut Workmen's Compensation Act was passed in 1913, three years after the adoption of the first American state workmen's compensation law in New York, and that the corresponding Swiss law was approved by the Federal Assembly in 1911. Furthermore, it is important to note that the Roman law tradition, which is the most distinctive common characteristic of the Civil Law systems, had less influence in Switzerland than in other parts of continental Europe.[5] Consequently, should an analysis of Swiss cases reveal contrasts to adjudication in Common Law systems, it can be expected that even more acute contrasts would be encountered in a comparison involving a Civil Law jurisdiction in which the impact of Roman law was more dominant.

Before proceeding to a comparative analysis of Connecticut and Swiss workmen's compensation cases, some comments that describe the administration of Swiss workmen's compensation seem appropriate.[6] During the second half of the nineteenth century, several federal laws were passed that imposed liability on employers for injuries of employees in specified industries. The first comprehensive federal law, which, with subsequent amendments, is still the controlling law in the field of workmen's compensation, was adopted in 1911. Its name alone—Federal Law for Sickness and Accident Insurance—indicates that the law is more inclusive in scope than the workmen's compensation laws of the American states. This is true not only because the act contains provisions for health insurance but also because the accident insurance covers injuries that are related or—subject to some limitations—unrelated to the employment. On the other hand, some forms of employment are excluded. For the purpose of administering accident insurance, the act of 1911 created the Swiss Accident Insurance Institute, with a central office in Lucerne and regional offices in the various cantons. Although the Institute is not an integral part of the federal administration, it is a public institution, supervised by the federal government. The members of its Board of Management are elected by the Federal Council. The functions of the Institute reveal another contrast to the administration of workmen's compensation in the United States. It is the institution through which, on the one hand, employers are insured for injuries of their employees, and which, on the other hand, originally determines the validity

[5] See René David, *Einführung in die grossen Rechtssysteme der Gegenwart*, Deutsche Übersetzung und Bearbeitung von Günther Grasmann (Munich and Berlin: C. H. Beck'sche Verlagbuchhandlung, 1966), p. 58.

[6] See Alfred Maurer, *Recht und Praxis der schweizerischen obligatorischen Unfallversicherung*, Zweite Auflage (Bern: Verlag Stämpfli, 1963), and Jean-Daniel Ducommun, "Le Cinquantenaire du Tribunal Fédéral des Assurances," *Schweizerische Zeitschrift für Sozialversicherung*, 11. Jahrgang, Heft 2 (1967), 241–55.

of claims of employees. The Swiss Accident Insurance Institute thus combines the functions of the insurance company and the workmen's compensation agency, which are clearly separated in the American states. Furthermore, only in less than one-fifth of the American states is workmen's compensation insurance exclusively public, and only in approximately another fifth of the states is an option of public insurance available.

For the purpose of judicial review of the decisions of the Swiss Accident Insurance Institute, the federal act of 1911 gave each canton the responsibility of designating one of its courts as a tribunal for adjudicating disputes between claimants and the Institute and related controversies. The jurisdiction of these courts is comparable to the review of decisions of American workmen's compensation cases by intermediate state appellate courts or by state courts of original general trial jurisdiction. For the purpose of final review, however, the act of 1911 created a special federal court consisting of five judges (seven since the beginning of 1970), who are elected by the Federal Assembly for a period of six years. This court is known as the Federal Insurance Court, located in Lucerne, and now is a division of the Swiss Federal Court. Consequently, a further appeal from the decisions of the cantonal courts is directed to a federal court and not to an appellate court of the canton. This arrangement differs, therefore, from the final review of American state workmen's compensation cases by state supreme courts.

On the basis of the provisions of the act of 1911, the Federal Insurance Court was organized by the Federal Assembly in 1917, and it began to adjudicate cases in 1918. In addition to the review of accident insurance cases from the cantonal courts, the Federal Court also has jurisdiction in cases involving military insurance, old age and survivors' insurance, subsidies to families in agriculture, unemployment compensation, compensation of persons in military service for loss of income, insurance for invalids, sickness insurance, and supplements under old age and survivors' and invalids' insurance. In all cases the Court has final jurisdiction. Since this study is concerned with accident insurance cases relating to employment, it should be noted that some actions of the Swiss Accident Insurance Institute are not subject to review by the Federal Insurance Court. Regulations of the Institute regarding the prevention of industrial accidents and occupational diseases can be appealed first to the Federal Office for Social Insurance and then to the Swiss Federal Court in Lausanne. Actions of the Institute with regard to physicians or pharmacists are adjudicated without further appeal by special courts in the cantons (*Schiedsgerichte*), which are not identical with the cantonal courts that review disputes between the Institute and employees. Finally, there are actions of the Institute, such as actions involving its own personnel, for which the Institute is liable in the ordinary courts. None of these actions involve disputes between claimants for compensation and the Institute. In such disputes, the Federal Insurance Court has final jurisdiction.

The cases which are reviewed by the Swiss Federal Court in the field of accident insurance and involve injuries related to the employment are the counterpart of the American workmen's compensation cases that are reviewed by state courts. They include occupational diseases. It is the comparison of the decisions of the Swiss Federal Court in these cases with the corresponding decisions of the Supreme Court of Connecticut that is the subject of this study. In spite of the fact that the Common Law rules regarding employers' liability are not used in the adjudication of workmen's compensation cases, the Supreme Court of Connecticut is a tribunal which functions in the Common Law tradition. Correspondingly, the procedures of the Swiss Federal Insurance Court have remained within the general tradition of the Civil Law systems, even though it is concerned with specialized areas of administrative law.[7] Consequently, the two tribunals have the characteristics of their respective legal systems that make a comparison appropriate.

Since this comparison is concerned with the analysis of judicial decisions as functions of controlling facts, reports of the applicable cases had to be studied. Swiss court reports are not as extensively published as American court reports. For the Connecticut workmen's compensation cases, the transcripts of the workmen's compensation commissioners' hearings, their findings, the reasons of claimants or respondents for appeal, the decisions of the Superior Court, and the briefs of claimants and respondents to the Supreme Court are published in the *Connecticut Supreme Court Records and Briefs*, in addition to the opinions of the Supreme Court in the *Connecticut Reports*. The information for the analysis of the relevant Connecticut cases, which the Supreme Court had decided since the adoption of the State Workmen's Compensation Act of 1913, could be obtained, therefore, entirely from published records. For the Swiss workmen's compensation cases, on the other hand, considerable reliance had to be placed on unpublished records, which are kept in excellent condition in the library and archives of the Federal Insurance Court in Lucerne. Through the generous cooperation of the judges and staff of the Court, these records were made available for the purpose of this research. Selected decisions of the Federal Insurance Court are published in the Official Collection (*Amtliche Sammlung*) as *Entscheidun-*

---

[7] See Maurer, *op. cit.*, p. 377.

gen des Eidgenössischen Versicherungsgerichts. This collection is available in the United States in at least two libraries (the Library of Congress and the Harvard Law Library). The decisions of the cantonal courts in accident insurance cases usually are not published. All the cases that have been reviewed by the Federal Court since 1918 are preserved in unpublished form in the archives of the Court at Lucerne. They were examined at the Court for the purpose of this study. Moreover, the original decisions of the Swiss Accident Insurance Institute also are available in unpublished form at the central office of the Institute in Lucerne. From 1918 to 1936 all decisions of the Federal Insurance Court appeared in an unpublished series, known as the Internal Collection (*Interne Sammlung*), all copies of which are kept at the Court in Lucerne. During that period, the Official Collection was the only selective series. In 1936 the Internal Collection became a second, more extensive selective series, and decisions which were not reported in either the published Official Collection or in the unpublished Internal Collection became memoranda without opinions. In this study, all decisions in the accident insurance cases related to employment (the other cases would not be comparable to workmen's compensation) that appear (1) in the Official Collection from 1918 to 1936, (2) in the Official Collection from 1936 to the present time, and (3) in the Internal Collection from 1936 to the present time were included. The cases that appear in the Internal Collection from 1918 to 1936 are for the purpose of this analysis identical with the cases in the Official Collection during that period; for this reason, they were not included in this study. Furthermore, the decisions in the form of memoranda from 1936 to the present time are in content duplicates of the decisions in the Official Collection and in the Internal Collection during that period; consequently, they also were excluded from the study. As a result, 236 cases were obtained for the purpose of this study.

Adjudication in a Common Law System —
Initial Assumption of a Linear Function

In the review of workmen's compensation cases, the decisions of the Supreme Court of Connecticut depend on relevant facts. These facts are listed in Table 1.1. Speaking in mathematical terms, it can be said that the decisions are functions of the facts. Although different combinations of these facts determine whether the decision of the Court is in favor of the claimant or against him, none of these facts constitutes an indispensable condition for a favorable decision.[8] For this reason, it was pointed out in a previous study [9] that initially a linear model has to be assumed in representing these decisions. A simple hypothetical example will illustrate this point.

Assume that—contrary to reality—the justices of the Supreme Court of Connecticut consider only two facts in deciding a workmen's compensation case: X_1 and X_2, with respective weights of b_1 and b_2. Assume, furthermore, that the decision is represented by Y and that a is a constant. If the decision in any case is regarded as a function of the two facts, it would be represented by the following equation:

$$(1) \qquad a + b_1X_1 + b_2X_2 = Y.$$

The equation is linear, for in three-dimensional space it can be represented by a plane. If only one fact were involved, it would be represented by a line, and if more than two facts were involved it would be represented by a hyperplane. In each instance, an additive relationship between the facts exists. As this model is applied to *all* the facts in *all* Connecticut workmen's compensation cases that were examined, the following system of equations is obtained:

$$(2) \quad \begin{aligned} a + b_1X_{11} + b_2X_{12} + \cdots + b_jX_{1j} + \cdots + b_{22}X_{1,22} + e_1 &= Y_1 \\ a + b_1X_{21} + b_2X_{22} + \cdots + b_jX_{2j} + \cdots + b_{22}X_{2,22} + e_2 &= Y_2 \\ \cdots \qquad\qquad\qquad\qquad\qquad\qquad & \\ a + b_1X_{k1} + b_2X_{k2} + \cdots + b_jX_{kj} + \cdots + b_{22}X_{k22} + e_k &= Y_k \\ \cdots \qquad\qquad\qquad\qquad\qquad\qquad & \\ a + b_1X_{128,1} + b_2X_{128,2} + \cdots + b_jX_{128j} + \cdots + b_{22}X_{128,22} + e_{128} & \\ &= Y_{128.} \end{aligned}$$

These simultaneous equations apply to the 22 facts listed in Table 1.1 and their weights ($j = 1, 2, \ldots, 22$) in the 128 cases which were examined ($k = 1, 2, \ldots, 128$). Each numerical value of X_{kj} (0, 1, or an integer larger than 1), which indicates the absence, presence, or several manifestations of fact j in case k, is known. The numerical value of Y_k (0, 1, \ldots, 5), which represents the number of votes of the justices supporting a decision in favor of the claimant in case k (and consequently

---

[8] It is true that the Connecticut Workmen's Compensation Act does not permit compensation for injuries caused by consumption of alcoholic beverages or narcotics (*General Statutes of Connecticut, Revision of 1958*, Sec. 31–275). Since, however, such cases never have reached the Supreme Court, this fact has not become an indispensable condition in adjudication. Furthermore, Sec. 31–294 requires the reporting of an accident or occupational diseases within a year. But no case has been reviewed by the Court in which this period has been exceeded.

[9] See *supra*, note 3.

Table 1.1.   Facts in the Connecticut workmen's compensation cases

---

Status of the injury as an occupational disease or as a result of repetitive trauma or repetitive acts

1. Injury consists of a disease or a physical disability which is frequently encountered in the occupation of the employee.
2. Injury consists of a disease or a physical disability which reasonably can be connected with the occupation of the employee.

Circumstances under which an accident or an act alleged to have caused the injury occurred

3. Accident or act occurred during working hours.
4. Accident or act occurred in the course of an activity known to and permitted by the employer, or customary and not forbidden by the employer.
5. Accident or act occurred in the course of an activity conducive to efficient work.
6. Accident or act occurred in the course of an activity indispensable to the performance of the work.
7. Accident or act occurred on the premises of employment, in an area annexed to the place of employment, in an area where the work normally is performed, in the direct course of transportation furnished by the employer, or in living accommodations furnished by the employer.
8. Accident occurred as the result of an act or activity which did not involve unnecessary, self-imposed, knowingly hazardous conduct, such as taking a "joy ride" on a conveyor belt for unloading coal.
9. Accident occurred as the result of an act by the injured employee, the occurrence of which was known to the employer and not effectively forbidden.

Circumstances under which the injury became known

10. Injury became immediately apparent to the employee as a result of an accident or act.
11. Accident or act as described by the claimant was observed by other persons.
12. Injury became immediately apparent to other observers as a result of an accident or act.
13. Injury was reported to the employer as soon as it became apparent to the employee.
14. Accident or act alleged to have caused the injury was promptly reported to the employer.
15. Accident or act alleged to have caused the injury was brought to the attention of a physician when medical treatment for the injury was first sought.
16. Claim for compensation was filed as soon as the injury became apparent to the employee.

Conditions of the employment which affect the probability of an injury subject to compensation

17. Conditions of employment exposed employee to an uncommon risk or to a common risk to an unusual degree, or to an exertion or risk beyond usual workaday labor (including railroad crossings en route to work and adjacent to the place of employment when employer knows of and permits use of crossing path).

Table 1.1.   Facts in the Connecticut workmen's compensation cases (*continued*)

Casual aspects of the injury

18. The cause alleged by the claimant is the probable cause of the injury, as supported by expert testimony.
19. The injury is causally traceable to the employment other than through weakened resistance or lowered vitality, as supported by expert testimony.
20. The accident or act is the cause of the injury, and no expert testimony is necessary to establish this fact.

Evidence not derived from expert testimony

21. There were no contradictions in the evidence given by the claimant.
22. All evidence not derived from expert testimony was in favor of the validity of the allegation made by the claimant.

---

indicates whether the decision is in favor of the claimant or against him), also is known. The term e_k represents a residual which accounts in the case for the difference between the observed Y_k and the estimated Y_k. The only unknowns are the weights of the facts b_j and the constant a, which are obtained by solving the equations by the method of least squares.

The additive relationships between facts imply that there is no fact that must be present in a case as an indispensable condition for a decision in favor of the claimant. Any fact can be absent in a case decided in favor of the claimant, provided that the combination of the facts that are present is sufficient for such a decision in terms of the weights of the facts. The underlying logical relationship can be represented as

$$(3) \qquad D_{pro} \rightarrow X_1 \lor X_2 \lor \ldots \lor X_{22}.$$

D_{pro} in this statement means that the decision is in favor of the claimant, $\rightarrow$ represents the conditional *if . . . then*, and $\lor$ denotes disjunction *or*, but—more specifically—one, several, or all of the terms connected by the symbol. Accordingly, the only condition that is imposed on a decision in favor of the claimant is that at least one of the facts be present. Of course, the fact that this condition has been met does not necessarily mean that the decision will be in favor of the claimant. Such a decision merely is logically possible; on empirical grounds, it is unlikely.

An examination of the workmen's compensation cases decided by the Supreme Court of Connecticut shows that the Court has neither specified nor used any of the controlling facts as an indispensable condition for a decision in favor of the claimant. Since the absence of such a condition is properly reflected in a linear model, characterized by the indicated additive relationships between facts, such a model had to be initially assumed. Further investigation showed that a nonlinear model, with multiplicative relationships between some of the controlling facts, represents the decisions more accurately.[10] On that basis, the system of equations (2) has to be restated in the following form:

$$a + b_1X_{11} + b_2X_{12} + \cdots + (1 + b_4X_{14})(1 + b_{18}X_{1,18}) + b_5X_{15}$$
$$+ \cdots + (1 + b_7X_{17})(1 + b_{20}X_{1,20}) + b_8X_{18} + \cdots + b_{17}X_{1,17}$$
$$+ b_{19}X_{1,19} + b_{21}X_{1,21} + b_{22}X_{1,22} + e_1 = Y_1$$

$$a + b_1X_{21} + b_2X_{22} + \cdots + (1 + b_4X_{24})(1 + b_{18}X_{2,18}) + b_5X_{25}$$
$$+ \cdots + (1 + b_7X_{27})(1 + b_{20}X_{2,20}) + b_8X_{28} + \cdots + b_{17}X_{2,17}$$
$$+ b_{19}X_{2,19} + b_{21}X_{2,21} + b_{22}X_{2,22} + e_2 = Y_2$$

(4) . . . .

$$a + b_1X_{k1} + b_2X_{k2} + \cdots + (1 + b_4X_{k4})(1 + b_{18}X_{k18}) + b_5X_{k5}$$
$$+ \cdots + (1 + b_7X_{k7})(1 + b_{20}X_{k20}) + b_8X_{k8} + \cdots + b_{17}X_{k17}$$
$$+ b_{19}X_{k19} + b_{21}X_{k21} + b_{22}X_{k22} + e_k = Y_k$$

. . . .

$$a + b_1X_{128,1} + b_2X_{128,2} + \cdots + (1 + b_4X_{128,4})(1 + b_{18}X_{128,18})$$
$$+ b_5X_{128,18} + \cdots + (1 + b_7X_{128,7})(1 + b_{20}X_{128,20}) + b_8X_{128,8}$$
$$+ \cdots + b_{17}X_{128,17} + b_{19}X_{128,19} + b_{21}X_{128,21} + b_{22}X_{128,22} + e_{128}$$
$$= Y_{128}.$$

The multiplicative relationships between $(1 + b_4X_{k4})$ and $(1 + b_{18}X_{k18})$ and $(1 + b_7X_{k7})$ and $(1 + b_{20}X_{k20})$ introduce nonlinearities into the equations that originally were represented by a hyperplane. Consequently, the newly obtained function is nonlinear. It should be noted, however, that even this nonlinear function does not incorporate the presence of any fact as an indispensable condition for a decision in favor of the claimant. Consider, for example, the multiplicative relationship between facts 4 and 18:

$$(5) \qquad \cdots + (1 + b_4X_{k4})(1 + b_{18}X_{k18}) + \cdots = Y_k.$$

On the basis of this multiplicative relationship, the presence of fact 18 ($X_{18} = 1$) could increase the impact of fact 4 on the decision. In the absence of fact 18 ($X_{18} = 0$), however, fact 4 still would influence the decision. The same observation applies to facts 7 and 20. It is in this respect that the nonlinear function which applies to the Swiss cases is decisively different.

Adjudication in a Civil-Law System—A Nonlinear Function

An examination of the decisions of the Swiss Federal Insurance Court in accident cases shows that there are facts that must be present in a case as

[10] See *supra*, note 3.

indispensable conditions for a decision in favor of the claimant. It has been seen that such conditions do not exist in the comparable Connecticut cases. In the Swiss cases, however, there are several facts that have this characteristic. These facts, which appear in Table 1.2, now will be examined.

On the basis of provisions of the Sickness and Accident Insurance Act of 1911, the Swiss Federal Council defines occupational diseases. Consequently, the fact that a disease has been designated as an occupational disease by the Council (fact 1) is an indispensable condition for a possible decision in favor of the claimant, if a claim invoking such a disease has been made. A similar condition does not exist in the adjudication of the Connecticut workmen's compensation cases. The fact that a physical disability is frequently encountered in an occupation, or that it can be reasonably connected with the employment, is a leading consideration for the Supreme Court of Connecticut, but the Court is not limited to even one of these two facts in accepting a disease as occupational.

Fact 1 constitutes an indispensable condition for a possible decision in favor of the claimant by virtue of legislative prescription. Other important facts that represent such conditions have not been specified by the Legislature but by the Federal Insurance Court. In this manner, the Court has imposed indispensable conditions on its own decision-making process. Facts 2 to 5 in Table 1.2 are of this nature. They specify that a a compensable accident must have been caused by an external factor, which must be unusual, must have a sudden impact on the human body, and must have a damaging effect. Each of these characteristics involving an accident must be present in a case in order to allow the Court to render a decision in favor of the claimant. Furthermore, both in occupational disease cases and accident cases, the damaging effects must not have been intended by the claimant.

Before other facts are discussed, it should be noted how facts that constitute an indispensable condition for a decision in favor of the claimant can be represented in an equation. A consideration of the initial hypothetical example and equation (1), with modifications, will be helpful. Assume that—contrary to reality—the judges of the Swiss Federal Insurance Court consider only two facts in deciding an accident insurance case: X_1 and X_2, with respective weights b_1 and b_2. Assume, furthermore, that the decision is represented by Y, and that the constant a, which was used in equation (1), is 0. Finally, assume that the presence of both fact 1 and fact 2 constitutes an indispensable condition for a decision in favor of the claimant. The decision then would be represented by

(6) $$(b_1X_1)(b_2X_2) = Y.$$

Table 1.2. Facts in the Swiss workmen's compensation cases

General characteristic of occupational diseases

1. The injury consists of a disease alleged to have been caused directly or indirectly by a substance or harmful exposure included by the Swiss Federal Council in the list of occupational diseases under Art. 68, Sec. 1 of the *KUVG* [*Kranken- und Unfallversicherung Gesetz* (Sickness and Accident Insurance Law), a part of which is the Swiss workmen's compensation law], or of a disease designated as an occupational disease by the Federal Council on the basis of Art. 68, Sec. 3 of the *KUVG*.

General characteristics of the accident or act alleged to have caused the injury

2. In connection with the alleged accident, an external factor had an impact on the human body (without causing an occupational disease). The nature of that factor was mechanical, electrical, radioactive, or consisted of the entering of water into the respiratory system, a detonation, or a motion which led to an injury. The factor originated externally (or in the mouth), and the injury is external or internal.

3. The external factor was more or less of unusual nature, e.g., it did not consist of bacteria or a virus (with the exception of specified infections), not of a deteriorating influence on bones and joints, and not of coal dust causing an irritation of the eyes.

4. The external factor had a sudden impact on the human body, i.e., it had a single impact—such as would be caused by a fall, a blow, a shot, ionized rays, high or low temperatures, heatstroke, or sunstroke—but not several, repeated, small impacts.

5. The external factor had a damaging effect on the human body, in a physical or psychological sense, or caused damage to artificial limbs or other artificial body aids, while the latter were attached to the human body and an injury to the person in the physical or psychological sense also occurred.

6. The damaging effect of the external factor or of the substance alleged to have caused an occupational disease was not intended by the claimant.

Circumstances under which the accident or act alleged to have caused the injury occurred

7. The alleged accident or act occurred (a) in the course of work which the claimant performed in accordance with an order of the employer, (b) in the course of an activity which was in the interest of the employer and for which the claimant could assume the consent of the employer, or (c) during a recess at work or before or after working hours, while the claimant was authorized to be on the premises of employment or in an area in which he was exposed to the hazards of the employment (Art. 67, Sec. 2 of the *KUVG*).

Circumstances under which the accident or act alleged to have caused the injury and its consequences became known *

8. The alleged accident, act, or occupational disease was reported to the employer or the Swiss Accident Insurance Institute within three months. (This fact refers to the provisions for delay in reporting in Art. 70 of the *KUVG*.)

9. The claimant made statements about the alleged accident or act that did

Table 1.2. Facts in the Swiss workmen's compensation cases
(*continued*)

---

      not contain contradictions to an extent that they cannot be disregarded in the interest of a consistent administration of accident insurance.

10. The alleged accident or act appears certain or highly probable on the basis of expert testimony or other evidence.

Former compensation

11. The claimant alleges an occupational disease, and he did not receive compensation for exposure to cement or calcium hydroxide during the past five years for a period of at least 150 days (Executive Order of the Swiss Federal Council of November 11, 1952, Art. 2).

Causal aspects of the injury

12. It is probable that the harmful substance or exposure, which has been included by the Federal Council in the list of occupational diseases, did not merely have an unfavorable influence, but that it was the primary cause of the occupational disease, in the sense that it contributed more to the disease than any combination of all other causes.

13. It is probable that the harmful substance or exposure, which has been included by the Federal Council in the list of occupational diseases, was the primary cause of the disease in the sense that its legally recognized impact during employment in Switzerland was greater than its impact during employment in other countries. Furthermore, an international agreement like the treaty with Italy of December 14, 1962 (equating employment in Italy to Swiss employment) is not applicable in this instance.

14. It is probable that the listed harmful substance or exposure, which has been included by the Federal Council in the list of occupational diseases, was the primary cause of the disease in the sense that its legally recognized impact in the course of employment was greater than any previous or subsequent impact not connected with employment.

15. The claimant suffers from a disease to which an acknowledged occupational disease contributed at least to some legally relevant degree.

16. On the basis of expert testimony, it is certain or highly probable that the alleged accident or act caused the injury.

17. On the basis of expert testimony, greater probability or plausibility can be attributed to the assumption that the injury was caused by the alleged accident or act than to the opposite assumption. It is not certain or highly probable, however, that the alleged accident or act caused the injury.

18. The consequences of the injury impair the employability of the claimant, necessitate medical treatment beyond the one already received, or have caused the death of the claimant.

---

    * In contrast to procedures employed by American state supreme courts, the Swiss Federal Insurance Court has the authority to order new expert testimony and a complete resubmission of evidence before its own examiner. For this reason, the Swiss Court does not give in its opinions as much detailed attention to the circumstances of the accident as the American courts do, which—for the purpose of evidence—depend entirely on the lower court records and the appellate briefs.

This function is nonlinear, for in three-dimensional space it is not represented by a plane but by a hull. If fact 1 is absent in a case represented by this function, X_1 is 0, and the entire left side of the equation would vanish even if fact 2 were present ($X_2 = 1$). Y then also would be 0, indicating a decision against the claimant. It can be seen, therefore, that this equation represents fact 1 and fact 2 as indispensable conditions for a decision in favor of the claimant. Since the constant a has been set equal to 0, the hull that represents the function passes through the origin.

It should be noted that the implication of the multiplicative relationship between facts in equation (6) is quite different from the one encountered in the Connecticut cases. Consider again, for example, equation (5). If fact 4 is absent in a case ($X_4 = 0$), the left side of the equation does not vanish, i.e., the impact of fact 4 on the decision is unimpaired, and Y does not become 0. Consequently, unlike equation (6), equation (5) does not represent either fact 4 or fact 18 as an indispensable condition for a decision in favor of the claimant.

Assume now—still contrary to reality—that the decisions of the Swiss Federal Insurance Court depend only on the facts that already have been discussed, namely, facts 1 to 6, as listed in Table 1.2. By applying the model of equation (6), the decision of the Court in a case then would have to be represented by

(7) $[b_1X_1 + (b_2X_2)(b_3X_3)(b_4X_4)(b_5X_5)]b_6X_6 = Y.$

This function allows the possibility that the case may involve an occupational disease or an accident. Should the former be true, the values of X_2 to X_5 would be 0, since an accident did not occur. Should the latter apply, X_1 would be 0, since an occupational disease is not under consideration. In neither of these situations would the left side of the equation vanish. This attribute of the equation is desired, for it cannot be expected that an occupational disease case involves an accident, and vice versa. However, if either fact 1 (designation of the disease as occupational by the Federal Council) or fact 6 (unintentional injury) is absent in an occupational disease case, a decision in favor of the claimant is precluded, for both facts constitute indispensable conditions for such a decision. Likewise, if any of facts 2 to 5 (referring to the characteristics of the accident) or fact 6 is absent in a case involving an accident, a decision in favor of the claimant also is precluded. In these instances, the left side of the equation vanishes as a result of the multiplicative relationships between the applicable values of X, which become 0. Y then also becomes 0. A multiplicative relationship exists not only between fact 1 and fact 6 and facts 2 to 5 combined and fact 6 but also among facts 2 to 5. This relationship is necessary, for each of the latter facts must be present in an accident case as an indispensable condition for a decision in favor of the claimant. The underlying logical relationship for equation (7) can be represented as

(8) $\qquad D_{pro} \rightarrow [X_1 \lor (X_2 \land X_3 \land X_4 \land X_5)] \land X_6.$

The notation is the same as in statement (3), with the addition of $\land$, denoting conjunction *and*. In comparing (7) and (8), it can readily be seen that an additive relationship corresponds to disjunction, and that a multiplicative relationship is the counterpart of conjunction. As has been noted earlier, the fact that the indispensable conditions have been met does not necessarily mean that the decision will be in favor of the claimant; it means only that such a decision is possible.

The same basic considerations apply to extending equation (7) to the other relevant facts. For accident insurance cases, the statutory provisions specify the circumstances under which the accident or harmful act must have occurred (fact 7). These circumstances must be included in equation (7) in the following form:

(9) $\qquad [b_1 X_1 + (b_2 X_2)(b_3 X_3)(b_4 X_4)(b_5 X_5)(b_7 X_7)]b_6 X_6 = Y.$

In establishing an indispensable condition for a decision in favor of the claimant, these circumstances provide alternatives. The alleged accident or harmful act must have occurred at work, in the course of an activity in the interest of the employer, with the consent of the employer, or during a time close to working hours with authorization of the employee to be on the premises. If none of these alternatives is met, X_7 is 0, and the entire left side of the equation vanishes, since X_1 in an accident case also is 0. It is in this sense that the circumstances under which the accident or harmful act occurred constitute an indispensable condition for a possible decision in favor of the claimant.

A further extension of equation (7) is necessary for including facts that —with one exception—do not have to be present in a case as an indispensable condition for a decision in favor of the claimant:

(10) $\qquad [b_1 X_1 + (b_2 X_2)(b_3 X_3)(b_4 X_4)(b_5 X_5)(b_7 X_7)]b_6 X_6 [1 + b_8 X_8 + b_{10} X_{10}$
$\qquad\qquad\qquad\qquad\qquad + b_{11} X_{11}]b_9 X_9 = Y.$

As can be seen from the description in Table 1.2, facts 8 to 11 pertain to the circumstances under which the accident or harmful act become known and—in case of an occupational disease—to former compensation. With the exception of fact 9, none of these facts represents an indispensable condition for a decision in favor of the claimant. Consequently, the relationship between these facts must be additive. A constant of 1 has to be added, in order to avoid a 0 value for the expression containing these facts and a resulting 0 value for the entire left side of the equation. However, fact 9, which refers to the absence of serious contradictions in the allegations of the claimant, has to be present in a case as an indispensable condition for a decision in favor of the claimant. Consequently, its relationship to all other terms in the equation must be multiplicative.

Finally, the facts referring to the causal aspects of the injury (facts 12 to 18 in Table 1.2) have to be included in the equation:

$$(11) \quad [b_1X_1 + (b_2X_2)(b_3X_3)(b_4X_4)(b_5X_5)(b_7X_7)]b_6X_6[1 + b_8X_8 + b_{10}X_{10}$$
$$+ b_{11}X_{11}]b_9X_9[(b_{12}X_{12})(b_{13}X_{13})(b_{14}X_{14}) + b_{15}X_{15} + b_{16}X_{16}$$
$$+ b_{17}X_{17}]b_{18}X_{18} = Y.$$

The meaning of the additive and multiplicative relationships in the expression that has been added in equation (11) should be noted. In the case of an occupational disease, each of facts 12 to 14 or fact 15 must be present for a decision in favor of the claimant. If this condition is not met, the entire expression in the last set of brackets becomes 0, for the X-values of facts 16 and 17, which apply only to accidents, also are 0. The entire left side of the equation then vanishes, indicating a value of 0 for Y, i.e., a decision against the claimant. In a case involving an accident, facts 12 to 15 are not applicable, and the values of X_{12} to X_{15} therefore are 0. For a possible decision in favor of the claimant, fact 16 or 17 has to be present in the case. Otherwise the expression in the last set of brackets and the entire left side of the equation would vanish. Fact 18, referring to the consequences of the injury, must be present in all cases. Consequently, it has a multiplicative relationship to all other terms in the equation. It is in this sense that the Federal Insurance Court has specified the presence of facts referring to the causal aspects of the injury as indispensable conditions for decisions favorable to the claimant in occupational disease and accident cases.

For the reasons that have been indicated, equation (11) represents the most plausible nonlinear combination of facts for a decision of the Swiss Federal Court in any case that is the counterpart of an American workmen's compensation case. By employing the same notation as in statement (8), with 0 indicating "no fact" in a group, the underlying logical relationship for equation (11) can be represented as

$$(12) \quad D_{pro} \rightarrow [X_1 \vee (X_2 \wedge X_3 \wedge X_4 \wedge X_5 \wedge X_7)] \wedge X_6 \wedge [0 \vee X_8$$
$$\vee X_{10} \vee X_{11}] \wedge X_9 \wedge [(X_{12} \wedge X_{13} \wedge X_{14}) \vee X_{15} \vee X_{16}$$
$$\vee X_{17}] \wedge X_{18}.$$

In applying equation (11) to all 236 Swiss cases that have been examined, the following system of equations is obtained:

$$(13)$$

$$[b_1X_{11} + (b_2X_{12})(b_3X_{13})(b_4X_{14})(b_5X_{15})(b_7X_{17})]b_6X_{16}$$
$$[1 + b_8X_{18} + b_{10}X_{1,10} + b_{11}X_{1,11}]b_9X_{19}$$
$$[(b_{12}X_{1,12})(b_{13}X_{1,13})(b_{14}X_{1,14}) + b_{15}X_{1,15}$$
$$+ b_{16}X_{1,16} + b_{17}X_{1,17}]b_{18}X_{1,18} = Y_1$$
$$[b_1X_{21} + (b_2X_{22})(b_3X_{23})(b_4X_{24})(b_5X_{25})(b_7X_{27})]b_6X_{26}[1 + b_8X_{28}$$
$$+ b_{10}X_{2,10} + b_{11}X_{2,11}]b_9X_{29}[(b_{12}X_{2,12})(b_{13}X_{2,13})(b_{14}X_{2,14})$$
$$+ b_{15}X_{2,15} + b_{16}X_{2,16} + b_{17}X_{2,17}]b_{18}X_{2,18} = Y_2$$

$$\cdots\cdots\cdots\cdots\cdots\cdots\cdots\cdots\cdots\cdots$$

$$[b_1X_{k1} + (b_2X_{k2})(b_3X_{k3})(b_4X_{k4})(b_5X_{k5})(b_7X_{k7})]b_6X_{k6}[1 + b_8X_{k8}$$
$$+ b_{10}X_{k10} + b_{11}X_{k11}]b_9X_{k9}[(b_{12}X_{k12})(b_{13}X_{k13})(b_{14}X_{k14})$$
$$+ b_{15}X_{k15} + b_{16}X_{k16} + b_{17}X_{k17}]b_{18}X_{k18} = Y_k$$

$$\cdots\cdots\cdots\cdots\cdots\cdots\cdots\cdots\cdots\cdots$$

$$[b_1X_{236,1} + (b_2X_{236,2})(b_3X_{236,3})(b_4X_{236,4})(b_5X_{236,5})(b_7X_{236,7})]b_6X_{236,6}$$
$$[1 + b_8X_{236,8} + b_{10}X_{236,10} + b_{11}X_{236,11}]b_9X_{236,9}$$
$$[(b_{12}X_{236,12})(b_{13}X_{236,13})(b_{14}X_{236,14}) + b_{15}X_{236,15}$$
$$+ b_{16}X_{236,16} + b_{17}X_{236,17}]b_{18}X_{236,18} = Y_{236}.$$

This system of equations applies to the 18 facts in Table 1.2 and their weights ($j = 1, 2, \ldots, 18$) in the 236 cases that have been examined ($k = 1, 2, \ldots, 236$). Each numerical value of X_{kj} (0, 1, or an integer larger than 1), which indicates the absence, presence, or several manifestations of the fact j in case k, is known. The numerical value of Y_k, which represents the decision of the Court, is 1 if the decision is in favor of the claimant and 0 if the decision is against him. Values for Y_k in terms of the votes of the judges, which are appropriate for analyzing American court decisions, would not be meaningful for Swiss cases. Although the Swiss Federal Insurance Court consists of seven judges (the number was increased from five to seven at the beginning of 1970), there are no dissenting or concurring opinions. Not all decisions are made by the entire Court, but the number of justices who participate in a case is determined only by the amount in controversy. Each decision implies endorsement by the full Court. For this reason, Y has to be regarded as a dichotomous variable, indicating support of the contentions of the claimant by the entire Court ($Y_k = 1$) or denial of such support ($Y_k = 0$).

The unknowns in equations (13) are the weights of the facts, b_j ($j = 1, 2, \ldots, 18$). A solution of these equations for unique values of the b's is not possible. Since every b always appears in a multiplicative relationship with other b's, an infinite number of values for each b would satisfy the equations. This problem is not surmounted by an attempt to use the method of least squares for solving the equations. It should be noted that such a problem is not encountered in the solution of equations (4) for the Connecticut cases, for—as was shown earlier—the multiplicative relationships in that instance are different.

The indicated problem can be solved, however, by expanding equations (13) and by obtaining weights for the interactions (multiplicative relationships) between facts instead of weights for individual facts. To be sure, weights for interactions between facts alone are not as informative as weights for individual facts, especially because the latter—in their respective combinations—also constitute the former. Weights for the interactions between facts provide, however, the best possible information that can be obtained in this instance.

As each equation in (13) is expanded and $B_j(j = 1, 2, \ldots, 32)$ is substituted for each multiplicative combination of b's as a weight for each interaction between facts, the equations assume the following general form:

$$B_1 X_{k1} X_{k6} X_{k9} X_{k12} X_{k13} X_{k14} X_{k18} + B_2 X_{k1} X_{k6} X_{k9} X_{k15} X_{k18}$$
$$+ B_3 X_{k1} X_{k6} X_{k9} X_{k16} X_{k18}$$
$$+ B_4 X_{k1} X_{k6} X_{k9} X_{k17} X_{k18} + B_5 X_{k1} X_{k6} X_{k8} X_{k9} X_{k12} X_{k13} X_{k14} X_{k18}$$
$$+ B_6 X_{k1} X_{k6} X_{k8} X_{k9} X_{k15} X_{k18} + B_7 X_{k1} X_{k6} X_{k8} X_{k9} X_{k16} X_{k18}$$
$$+ B_8 X_{k1} X_{k6} X_{k8} X_{k9} X_{k17} X_{k18} + B_9 X_{k1} X_{k6} X_{k9} X_{k10} X_{k12} X_{k13} X_{k14} X_{k18}$$
$$+ B_{10} X_{k1} X_{k6} X_{k9} X_{k10} X_{k15} X_{k18} + B_{11} X_{k1} X_{k6} X_{k9} X_{k10} X_{k16} X_{k18}$$
$$+ B_{12} X_{k1} X_{k6} X_{k9} X_{k10} X_{k17} X_{k18} + B_{13} X_{k1} X_{k6} X_{k9} X_{k11} X_{k12} X_{k13} X_{k14} X_{k18}$$
$$+ B_{14} X_{k1} X_{k6} X_{k9} X_{k11} X_{k15} X_{k18} + B_{15} X_{k1} X_{k6} X_{k9} X_{k11} X_{k16} X_{k18}$$
$$+ B_{16} X_{k1} X_{k6} X_{k9} X_{k11} X_{k17} X_{k18}$$
$$+ B_{17} X_{k2} X_{k3} X_{k4} X_{k5} X_{k6} X_{k7} X_{k9} X_{k12} X_{k13} X_{k14} X_{k18}$$
$$+ B_{18} X_{k2} X_{k3} X_{k4} X_{k5} X_{k6} X_{k7} X_{k9} X_{k15} X_{k18}$$
$$+ B_{19} X_{k2} X_{k3} X_{k4} X_{k5} X_{k6} X_{k7} X_{k9} X_{k16} X_{k18}$$
$$(14) \quad + B_{20} X_{k2} X_{k3} X_{k4} X_{k5} X_{k6} X_{k7} X_{k9} X_{k17} X_{k18}$$
$$+ B_{21} X_{k2} X_{k3} X_{k4} X_{k5} X_{k6} X_{k7} X_{k8} X_{k9} X_{k12} X_{k13} X_{k14} X_{k18}$$
$$+ B_{22} X_{k2} X_{k3} X_{k4} X_{k5} X_{k6} X_{k7} X_{k8} X_{k9} X_{k15} X_{k18}$$
$$+ B_{23} X_{k2} X_{k3} X_{k4} X_{k5} X_{k6} X_{k7} X_{k8} X_{k9} X_{k16} X_{k18}$$
$$+ B_{24} X_{k2} X_{k3} X_{k4} X_{k5} X_{k6} X_{k7} X_{k8} X_{k9} X_{k17} X_{k18}$$
$$+ B_{25} X_{k2} X_{k3} X_{k4} X_{k5} X_{k6} X_{k7} X_{k9} X_{k10} X_{k12} X_{k13} X_{k14} X_{k18}$$
$$+ B_{26} X_{k2} X_{k3} X_{k4} X_{k5} X_{k6} X_{k7} X_{k9} X_{k10} X_{k15} X_{k18}$$
$$+ B_{27} X_{k2} X_{k3} X_{k4} X_{k5} X_{k6} X_{k7} X_{k9} X_{k10} X_{k16} X_{k18}$$
$$+ B_{28} X_{k2} X_{k3} X_{k4} X_{k5} X_{k6} X_{k7} X_{k9} X_{k10} X_{k17} X_{k18}$$
$$+ B_{29} X_{k2} X_{k3} X_{k4} X_{k5} X_{k6} X_{k7} X_{k9} X_{k11} X_{k12} X_{k13} X_{k14} X_{k18}$$
$$+ B_{30} X_{k2} X_{k3} X_{k4} X_{k5} X_{k6} X_{k7} X_{k9} X_{k11} X_{k15} X_{k18}$$
$$+ B_{31} X_{k2} X_{k3} X_{k4} X_{k5} X_{k6} X_{k7} X_{k9} X_{k11} X_{k16} X_{k18}$$
$$+ B_{32} X_{k2} X_{k3} X_{k4} X_{k5} X_{k6} X_{k7} X_{k9} X_{k11} X_{k17} X_{k18} = Y_k.$$

It should be noted again that equation (14) represents a whole system of equations, corresponding to (13). It would be appropriate to solve these equations for B by the method of least squares if Y were a continuous dependent variable. As already was indicated, however, Y is a dichotomous variable in this instance, with values of 1 or 0 (a decision in favor or against the claimant). Under these circumstances, a solution of the equations by the method of least squares, in the form of multiple regression analysis, would not be appropriate, for two reasons: (1) the expected value of the dependent variable would have to be in the interval (0, 1), regardless of the values of the independent variables; this condition is not compatible with the assumption that the expected value is a linear combination of the independent variables (although they represent in this instance a nonlinear function); (2) the assumption in multiple regression analysis that the distribution of the dependent variable around its expected value is independent of the level of that value does not apply to a dichotomous dependent variable.[11] Two-group discriminant analysis would be appropriate in this instance, if a linear combination of the independent variables could be assumed for locating the hyperplane that maximizes the separation of observations in the two categories. The important point here, however, is that the underlying relationship between the independent variables is nonlinear. It is true that multiple discriminant analysis includes nonlinear relationships. Since the dependent variable in question is dichotomous, only two-group discriminant analysis would be applicable.

In view of these considerations, a solution for the B's with Y as the dependent variable is not feasible in this instance. Another approach is possible, however, in which the independent variables are the same as in (14), but in which the dependent variable indicates the proportion of cases decided in favor of the claimant. If a consistent pattern in the decisions can be found on that basis, in terms of a significance test, the proposed relationship between the decisions and the independent variables can be accepted. This approach is known as probit analysis.[12] In

---

[11] See James Tobin, "The Application of Multivariate Probit Analysis to Economic Survey Data," Cowles Foundation Discussion Paper no. 1 (July 14, 1955, as revised Dec. 1, 1955), p. 2.

[12] See D. J. Finney, *Probit Analysis*, 2d ed. (Cambridge: At the University Press, 1952); Tobin, *op. cit.*; Arthur S. Goldberger, *Econometric Theory* (New York: Wiley, 1964), pp. 250–51. The exposition of probit analysis in this paper is based on Tobin's article but is different from it on some decisive points. Another important source of information is the article by Jerome Cornfield and Nathan Mantel, "Some New Aspects of the Application of Maximum Likelihood to the Calculation of the Dosage Response Curve," *Journal of the American Statistical Association*, XLV (June, 1950), pp. 181–210. See also John C. Blydenburgh, "Probit Analysis: A Method for Coping with Dichotomous Dependent Variables," *Social Sciences Quarterly*, LI (March,

this analysis, a continuous dependent variable I is a function of the independent variables, V_1, V_2, . . . , V_j, . . . , V_m, with weights, B_1, B_2, . . . , B_j, . . . , B_m, for an observation k:

$$(15) \quad I_k = B_0 + B_1V_{k1} + B_2V_{k2} + \cdots + B_jV_{kj} + \cdots + B_mV_{km}.$$

This linear combination can represent a nonlinear function, depending on the nature of V. Applied to equation (14), V_{kj} denotes the various products of the X_k's. Potentially, they are continuous variables, e.g., any number of accidents or external factors may be involved. Consequently, in this application, equation (15) does represent a nonlinear function. Since the values of the X_k's are known, the values of the V_k's also are known. The only unknowns for determining the value of I_k are the B's.

I is the probit of the proportion P of cases decided in favor of the claimant. Stated in general terms, I is the abscissa that corresponds to a probability P (cumulative densities) in a normal distribution with a mean of 5 and a variance of 1.

Accordingly,

$$(16a) \qquad P = P(I) = \frac{1}{\sqrt{2\pi}} \int_{-\infty}^{I-5} e^{-\frac{u^2}{2}} du$$

and

$$(16b) \qquad Q = Q(I) = 1 - P(I) = \frac{1}{\sqrt{2\pi}} \int_{I-5}^{\infty} e^{-\frac{u^2}{2}} du.$$

The cases represented by equation (15) can be combined into categories of identical observations. Equation (15) then becomes

$$(17) \quad I_i = B_0 + B_1V_{i1} + B_2V_{i2} + \cdots + B_jV_{ij} + \cdots + B_mV_{im},$$

where $i(i = 1, 2, \ldots, s)$ refers to any category of identical observations. For each category, n_i is the number of cases in that category, r_i is the number of cases in the category decided in favor of the claimant, and $n_i - r_i$ is the number of cases in the category decided against the claimant. The probabilities corresponding to (16) for each category are

$$(18a) \qquad P_i = P(I_i) = \frac{1}{\sqrt{2\pi}} \int_{-\infty}^{I_i-5} e^{-\frac{u^2}{2}} du$$

1971), pp. 889–99. In connection with the latter article, however, it should be carefully noted that the dependent variable in probit analysis (the proportion of observations falling into one of two categories) is continuous and *not* dichotomous. The phenomenon under consideration, *but not* the dependent variable as a function, is dichotomous. The author is indebted to Professor Gerald Kramer, Cowles Foundation and Department of Political Science, Yale University, for bringing probit analysis to his attention.

and

$$(18b) \qquad Q_i = Q(I_i) = \frac{1}{\sqrt{2\pi}} \int_{I_i-5}^{\infty} e^{-\frac{u^2}{2}} du.$$

The solution for the unknown B's is obtained in probit analysis by finding those values of the B's that—on the basis of the available observations—have maximum likelihood. Accordingly, the following likelihood function is formed:

$$L(B_0, B_1, \ldots, B_m)$$

$$(19) \qquad = \prod_{i=1}^{s} [P(B_0 + B_1 V_{i1} + \cdots + B_m V_{im})]^{r_i}$$

$$[Q(B_0 + B_1 V_{i1} + \cdots + B_m V_{im})]^{n_i-r_i}.$$

With substitutions from (17) and (18), (19) becomes

$$(20) \qquad L(B_0, B_1, \ldots, B_m) = \prod_{i=1}^{s} P_i{}^{r_i} Q_i{}^{n_i-r_i}.$$

In logarithmic form (20) can be stated as follows:

$$(21) \qquad \begin{aligned} L^*(B_0, B_1, \ldots, B_m) &= \log_e L(B_0, B_1, \ldots, B_m) \\ &= \sum_{i=1}^{s} [r_i \log_e P_i + (n_i - r_i)\log_e Q_i]. \end{aligned}$$

In order to maximize this function, its partial derivatives are taken with respect to every B and set equal to 0:

$$(22) \qquad \begin{aligned} f_0 &= \frac{\partial L^*}{\partial B_0} = 0 \\ f_1 &= \frac{\partial L^*}{\partial B_1} = 0 \\ & \cdot \quad \cdot \quad \cdot \quad \cdot \quad \cdot \quad \cdot \\ f_j &= \frac{\partial L^*}{\partial B_j} = 0 \\ & \cdot \quad \cdot \quad \cdot \quad \cdot \quad \cdot \quad \cdot \\ f_m &= \frac{\partial L^*}{\partial B_m} = 0, \end{aligned}$$

where

$$\frac{\partial L^*}{\partial B_j} = \sum_{i=1}^{s} \left[r_i V_{ij} \frac{Z_i}{P_i} - (n_i - r_i)V_{ij} \frac{Z_i}{Q_i} \right]$$

and

$$Z_i = \frac{\partial P_i}{\partial I_i} = \frac{1}{\sqrt{2\pi}} e^{-\frac{(I_i-5)^2}{2}}.$$

It should be noted again that by (17) I_i contains the unknowns B_0, $B_1, \ldots, B_m$. The equations in (22), therefore, are nonlinear. They can be solved by a method of iterative approximation, based on Taylor's theorem.[13] Initially, estimates of the unknowns, $B_0, B_1, \ldots, B_j, \ldots,$ B_m, are chosen. They can be designated as $C_0, C_1, \ldots, C_j, \ldots, C_m$. The differences between B_j and C_j, $(B_0 - C_0)$, $(B_1 - C_1)$, $\ldots,$ $(B_j - C_j), \ldots, (B_m - C_m)$ can be designated as $\Delta B_0, \Delta B_1, \ldots,$ $\Delta B_j, \ldots, \Delta B_m$, respectively. Since the values of B_j are not known, the values of ΔB_j also are unknown. By taking the partial derivatives of each normal equation f_j in equations (22) with respect to $B_0, B_1, \ldots,$ $B_j, \ldots, B_m$, and by substituting the initially chosen value of each C for each B, the following system of equations is formed:

$$f_0 + \frac{\partial f_0}{\partial B_0} \Delta B_0 + \frac{\partial f_0}{\partial B_1} \Delta B_1 + \cdots + \frac{\partial f_0}{\partial B_j} \Delta B_j + \cdots$$
$$+ \frac{\partial f_0}{\partial B_m} \Delta B_m = 0$$

$$f_1 + \frac{\partial f_1}{\partial B_0} \Delta B_0 + \frac{\partial f_1}{\partial B_1} \Delta B_1 + \cdots + \frac{\partial f_1}{\partial B_j} \Delta B_j + \cdots$$
$$+ \frac{\partial f_1}{\partial B_m} \Delta B_m = 0$$

(23) $\quad \cdot \quad \cdot \quad \cdot \quad \cdot \quad \cdot \quad \cdot \quad \cdot \quad \cdot \quad \cdot \quad \cdot \quad \cdot \quad \cdot \quad \cdot$

$$f_h + \frac{\partial f_h}{\partial B_0} \Delta B_0 + \frac{\partial f_h}{\partial B_1} \Delta B_1 + \cdots + \frac{\partial f_h}{\partial B_j} \Delta B_j + \cdots$$
$$+ \frac{\partial f_h}{\partial B_m} \Delta B_m = 0$$

$\quad \cdot \quad \cdot \quad \cdot \quad \cdot \quad \cdot \quad \cdot \quad \cdot \quad \cdot \quad \cdot \quad \cdot \quad \cdot \quad \cdot \quad \cdot$

$$f_m + \frac{\partial f_m}{\partial B_0} \Delta B_0 + \frac{\partial f_m}{\partial B_1} \Delta B_1 + \cdots + \frac{\partial f_m}{\partial B_j} \Delta B_j + \cdots$$
$$+ \frac{\partial f_m}{\partial B_m} \Delta B_m = 0,$$

where

$$\frac{\partial f_h}{\partial B_j} = \frac{\partial^2 L^*}{\partial B_j \partial B_h} = - \sum_{i=1}^{s} \left[r_i V_{ih} V_{ij} \left(\frac{I_i Z_i}{P_i} + \frac{Z_i^2}{P_i^2} \right) \right.$$
$$\left. + (n_i - r_i) V_{ih} V_{ij} \left(- \frac{I_i Z_i}{Q_i} + \frac{Z_i^2}{Q_i^2} \right) \right]$$

and $f_h = \dfrac{\partial L^*}{\partial B_h}$, as defined in (22).

[13] See, e.g., R. E. Johnson and F. L. Kiokemeister, *Calculus*, 3d ed. (Boston: Allyn & Bacon, 1964), pp. 397–401, and M. H. Protter and C. B. Morrey, Jr., *College Calculus* (Reading, Mass.: Addison-Wesley, 1964), pp. 695–99. For a detailed exposition of the application, see Kort, *op. cit.*, pp. 551–52.

Since the value of each C is substituted for each B in these equations, the only unknowns are ΔB_0, ΔB_1, . . . , ΔB_j, . . . , ΔB_m. Their values can be obtained by a direct solution of the equations, which is possible because the number of equations is equal to the number of unknowns. As the obtained values of ΔB_0, ΔB_1, . . . , ΔB_j, . . . , ΔB_m are added to the initially chosen values of C_0, C_1, . . . , C_j, . . . , C_m, the first approximation to B_0, B_1, . . . , B_j, . . . , B_m is found. The values of B_0, B_1, . . . , B_j, . . . , B_m in this first approximation then are used as new values for C_0, C_1, . . . , C_j, . . . , C_m, and the entire procedure is repeated as many times as is necessary for reaching a point at which the changes in the values of the C's become negligible.

In applying this method to the Swiss workmen's compensation cases as represented by equation (14), the following considerations were employed for choosing the initial value C_j for $B_j (j = 0, 1, 2, . . . , 32)$: as equation (14) was restated in the form of equation (17), it was found that the products V_3, V_4, V_7, V_8, V_9, V_{10}, V_{11}, V_{12}, V_{15}, V_{16}, V_{17}, V_{18}, V_{21}, V_{22}, V_{25}, V_{26}, V_{29}, V_{30}, V_{31}, V_{32} vanished for all observations (categories of cases). Accordingly, it seemed reasonable to assign initial values of 0 to C_3, C_4, C_7, C_8, C_9, C_{10}, C_{11}, C_{12}, C_{15}, C_{16}, C_{17}, C_{18}, C_{21}, C_{22}, C_{25}, C_{26}, C_{29}, C_{30}, C_{31}, C_{32}. A value of 0 also was initially assigned to C_0 for B_0, since in a case with all vanishing products $V_j (j = 1, 2, . . . , 32)$ B_0 also would be expected to be 0 (no impact on the decision). For all other C's for the B's, i.e., for C_1, C_2, C_5, C_6, C_{13}, C_{14}, C_{19}, C_{20}, C_{23}, C_{24}, C_{27}, C_{28}, initial values of 1 were assumed, in the absence of any indication at that point regarding the respective impacts of these coefficients as weights of the products V_j on the decisions.

Equations (23) were solved by the indicated iterative procedure, with the use of a high-speed computer. Remote communications terminals demonstrated their special advantages in this instance. The solutions that were obtained for the B's are listed in Table 1.3, and the corresponding values of I_i that then were computed in accordance with (17) are listed in Table 1.4.

The results shown in Table 1.4 should be interpreted in terms of the comments introduced with equation (17). The 236 cases that had been examined were combined into categories of identical cases. These categories are identified in column 1 of Table 1.4. Column 2 shows the number of cases in each category, column 3 indicates the number of cases in each category with decisions in favor of the claimants, and column 4 lists the number of cases with decisions against the claimants. The final values that were obtained for I_i, and thus for I_k, are shown in column 5. It will be noted that the values for I are comparatively large for those categories in which the cases were decided primarily in favor of the claimants, and are comparatively small for those categories in which the cases were primarily or exclusively decided against the claimants. The results suggest significance merely on the basis of inspection. This inference can be supported by a significance test.

For testing the significance of the results, the null hypothesis was used that I_k is independent of the V_k's, which are nonlinear combinations of

Table 1.3. Weights of interactions between facts in Swiss cases

	B_0	3.462		
B_1	−5.699		B_{17}	0.000
B_2	−0.465		B_{18}	0.000
B_3	0.000		B_{19}	−0.012
B_4	0.000		B_{20}	0.539
B_5	7.238		B_{21}	0.000
B_6	1.000		B_{22}	0.000
B_7	0.000		B_{23}	1.550
B_8	0.000		B_{24}	0.845
B_9	0.000		B_{25}	0.000
B_{10}	0.000		B_{26}	0.000
B_{11}	0.000		B_{27}	1.550
B_{12}	0.000		B_{28}	1.000
B_{13}	1.283		B_{29}	0.000
B_{14}	1.000		B_{30}	0.000
B_{15}	0.000		B_{31}	0.000
B_{16}	0.000		B_{32}	0.000

X_k's. By (19), the likelihood function in accordance with this hypothesis is

$$(24) \qquad L(B_0, 0, \ldots, 0) = [P(B_0)]^r [Q(B_0)]^{n-r},$$

where $r = \sum_{i=1}^{s} r_i$ and $n = \sum_{i=1}^{s} n_i$.

The value of B'_0 that maximizes this likelihood function is such that $P(B'_0) = r/n$. Consequently, the corresponding maximum likelihood function in logarithmic form is

$$(25) \quad L^*(B_0', 0, \ldots, 0) = r \log_e \frac{r}{n} + (n - r) \log_e \frac{n - r}{n}.$$

The following function then can be formed:

$$(26) \quad \log_e \lambda = L^*(B'_0, 0, \ldots, 0) - L^*(B_0, \ldots, B_m),$$

Table 1.4. Indices for cases

i	$n_i\left(\sum_{i=1}^{53} n_i = 236\right)$	r_i	$n_i - r_i$	I_i(final results)
1	33	31	2	6.551
2	5	4	1	5.846
3	1	0	1	3.462
4	28	3	25	3.462
5	10	2	8	3.462
6	1	0	1	3.462
7	1	0	1	3.462
8	12	1	11	3.462
9	1	0	1	3.462
10	10	1	9	3.462
11	1	0	1	3.462
12	2	1	1	5.001
13	5	0	5	3.462
14	10	2	8	3.462
15	3	0	3	3.462
16	2	0	2	3.462
17	40	2	38	3.462
18	2	1	1	5.001
19	9	0	9	3.462
20	10	9	1	6.284
21	4	0	4	3.462
22	1	0	1	3.462
23	1	0	1	3.462
24	1	0	1	3.462
25	1	0	1	3.462
26	2	0	2	3.462
27	1	0	1	3.462
28	1	0	1	3.462
29	3	0	3	3.462
30	2	0	2	3.462
31	1	0	1	3.462
32	1	0	1	3.462
33	4	0	4	3.462
34	1	0	1	3.462
35	2	1	1	5.001
36	1	0	1	3.462
37	1	0	1	3.462
38	2	0	2	3.462
39	1	0	1	3.462
40	2	0	2	3.462
41	3	0	3	3.462
42	1	0	1	3.462
43	1	0	1	3.462
44	1	0	1	3.462

Table 1.4.   Indices for cases (*continued*)

i	$n_i\left(\displaystyle\sum_{i=1}^{53} n_i = 236\right)$	r_i	$n_i - r_i$	I_i(final results)
45	1	0	1	−.954
46	2	1	1	4.998
47	1	0	1	3.462
48	2	1	1	5.001
49	2	0	2	3.462
50	1	0	1	3.462
51	1	0	1	3.462
52	1	0	1	3.462

where $L^*(B_0, B_1, \ldots, B_m)$ is the maximum likelihood function as defined in (21), with the values for $B_0, B_1, \ldots, B_m$ that were obtained as final results from the analysis. The function $-2 \log_e \lambda$ is distributed as a chi-square, with m degrees of freedom.[14] The value that was obtained for it in the analysis of the Swiss workmen's compensation cases is 144.715, with a chance probability $P < .001$. On that basis, the null hypothesis was rejected and the results were accepted as significant.

Conclusions

To some extent, the comparison of the Connecticut and Swiss workmen's compensation cases has shown a dependence on statutory sources in the decisions of the Swiss Federal Insurance Court. Such a dependence is not found in the decisions of the Supreme Court of Connecticut. Moreover, since Connecticut is representative of the administration of workmen's compensation in American states in various respects, this observation also can be made with regard to most American state courts. In this respect, the traditional belief that Civil Law systems rely more extensively on statutory sources than Common Law systems would be substantiated. Nevertheless, the impression should not be conveyed that the Swiss Federal Insurance Court ignores judicial precedent. On the contrary, it cites quite liberally its own decisions, with the characteristics of comparing and distinguishing precedent found in Common Law systems.

The important point, however, is that a more extensive dependence on

[14] See Alexander M. Mood and Franklin H. Graybill, *Introduction to the Theory of Statistics*, 2d ed. (New York: McGraw-Hill, 1963), p. 299.

statutory sources is not the decisive criterion for distinguishing Swiss adjudication of workmen's compensation from its American counterpart. The significant characteristic of adjudication is the imposition of conditions which the Federal Insurance Court considers indispensable in its decisions. Only a few of these conditions are specified by statute; most of them have been created by the Court. It is in this sense that Lawson's suggestion of the existence of a formal conceptual structure prior to the application of legal principles to decisions in Civil Law systems is re-reflected in the Swiss cases.[15] Moreover, Lawson's corresponding suggestion of a merely tentative conceptual framework in Common Law systems, subject to transformation into more concrete forms in the process of judicial experience, finds support in the Connecticut cases. The latter do not exhibit indispensable conditions analogous to the conditions in the Swiss cases. Without further qualifications, the proposed distinction between formal structure and a tentative framework in legal concepts would depend on intuitive judgment. However, it has been shown now that by employing linear and nonlinear functions this distinction can be stated in an unambiguous form in at least one area of adjudication in a Common Law system and a Civil Law system.

As already indicated, some convergence between American and Swiss workmen's compensation adjudication can be noted. Workmen's compensation is a part of administrative law, where similarities between Civil Law and Common Law systems exist. Furthermore, the reception of the Roman law, which is the most distinctive common characteristic of the Civil Law systems, had less influence in Switzerland than in other parts of continental Europe. Consequently, it can be expected that the differences in adjudication between American and Swiss workmen's compensation cases that have been revealed through the use of linear and nonlinear functions would become even more pronounced in the application of such functions to areas of law and jurisdictions where the historical contrasts between Common Law and Civil Law systems are even more acute.

Finally, it should be noted that the dependence of decisions on controlling facts or other relevant circumstances is a phenomenon which is not limited to the judicial process. Consequently, the analysis of decisions as linear and nonlinear functions of specified variables can be readily extended to decision-making processes beyond the framework of judicial action.

[15] See *supra*, notes 1 and 2.

A General Theory of the Calculus of Voting

2

Richard D. McKelvey,
University of Rochester, and
Peter C. Ordeshook,
Carnegie-Mellon University

Introduction

MUCH of the literature in electoral politics written before the publication of "A Theory of the Calculus of Voting" perverts the function of theory by relegating the decision to vote to the inexplicable world of the irrational.[1] That article, however, reexamines and rigorously reinterprets the voting act, revealing that both voting and abstaining are reasonable acts under respectively stated conditions. This earlier theory is inappropriate for multiparty contests, though, because its derivation assumes only two-candidate competition. We extend the voting calculus in this essay to permit inferences about participation in multicandidate elections. Specifically, we consider how a citizen might calculate the effect of his vote on the outcome in terms of: (1) the probabilities that his vote will materially affect outcomes, and (2) the utilities he associates with the election of alternative candidates.

We develop in Section 1 the decision-theoretic foundations for a general theory. We reconstruct in Section 2 the logic of the voting calculus for two-candidate contests, correcting an error in its original derivation. We develop (without proof) in Section 3 the implications of our general theory for three-candidate contests. We summarize these implications formally in Section 4 as a general theorem for any number of candidates. Additionally, we show that a series of paired comparisons between the

This research was supported by a grant from Resources for the Future, Inc., to Carnegie-Mellon University and from the National Science Foundation to the University of Rochester. The authors wish to thank Peter H. Aranson, Melvin J. Hinich, and Howard Rosenthal.

[1] William H. Riker and Peter C. Ordeshook, "A Theory of the Calculus of Voting," *American Political Science Review*, LXII (March, 1968), 25–42. See also Gordon Tullock, *Toward a Mathematics of Politics* (Ann Arbor: University of Michigan Press, 1968), chap. 7, and Anthony Downs, *An Economic Theory of Democracy* (New York: Harper and Row, 1957), 36–50, 260–76.

candidate for whom the citizen is likely to vote and the remaining candidates approximates the citizen's voting calculus. We construct in Section 5 a null model, with which we contrast the efficacy of voting in two- and in three-candidate contests by citizens who are totally ignorant about the probabilities of outcomes. We demonstrate, *ceteris paribus*, that for some citizens the efficacy of voting is greatest when two candidates compete, whereas for others this efficacy is greatest when three candidates compete. Finally, we consider in Section 6 the effects of varying degrees of competition in three-candidate contests. These effects supply a partial explanation for bandwagons: if the three candidates are closely matched, and if one candidate pulls slightly ahead of his competitors, the turnout among citizens who prefer this candidate increases. Because the proofs of our conclusions are tedious and mathematically complex we relegate them to appendixes.

1. Logical Foundations

We seek to generalize the voting calculus developed by Riker and Ordeshook, so we begin with an examination of their theory. Postulating that citizens maximize expected utility, and assuming that only two candidates compete, they demonstrate that the utility of voting less the utility of not voting can be expressed as

(1) $R = PB + D - C$

where:

   P is the probability that a citizen materially affects the outcome by
       voting;
   B is the differential utility that a citizen receives if his most preferred
       candidate wins, less the utility he receives if the opposition wins;
   C is the fixed cost a citizen incurs from voting;
   D is the utility a citizen derives from voting that is not dependent on
       his effect on the outcome;
   R is the expected utility a citizen receives from voting less the utility he
       receives from not voting. If $R > 0$, it is rational to vote, and if
       $R \leq 0$ it is irrational to do so.

Riker and Ordeshook illustrate empirically the necessity for the inclusion of the PB term, and their theoretical analysis suggests how P might be calculated. The analysis reveals that the objective value of P equals the probability that the citizen's vote is decisive. If the electorate is large, of course, this objective probability is exceedingly small. The authors suggest, nevertheless, that "for many people, the subjective estimate of P is higher than is reasonable, given the objective circumstances. Subjected to constant reminders that a few hundred carefully selected votes by nonvoters could reverse the results of very close elections . . . [P] may be as high as the propaganda urges it to be."[2] The implication is that, while citizens may apply various discount factors to compensate for the size of the electorate, the subjective value of P is a monotonically increasing function of its objective value. Empirical evidence is presented which suggests that at least some citizens actually behave as if they employ equation (1).

We cannot apply this analysis directly to multicandidate contests, however, because we cannot infer from it how a citizen might calculate the efficacy of his vote when the number of candidates exceeds two. A conclusion of "The Theory of the Calculus of Voting" is that the expected utility of voting is a function of the closeness of the election and of the differential utility between the two candidates. We cannot state, however, that this conclusion is true for multicandidate contests. Even if we were to assume a natural extension of equation (1), we cannot readily infer how citizens might calculate the closeness of the election or the differential utility among candidates in such contests. For two-candidate contests the meaning of closeness is relatively clear; but if the number of candidates exceeds two, the meaning is ambiguous. Are two elections equally close, for example, if in the first election two candidates are equally matched and the third candidate has little chance of success, but in the second election all three candidates conceivably can win although one candidate has a slight lead over his two opponents? Similarly, the extension of B is unclear for multicandidate contests. Are benefits greater when a citizen strongly prefers candidate 1 to candidates 2 and 3, and perceives no difference between 2 and 3, or if he perceives some differences among all three candidates?

The citizen's voting calculus, therefore, requires generalization; so we reconsider the logical foundations of the voting calculus. (We note, however, that our generalization applies only to elections in which a single candidate — the candidate who receives a plurality — wins. While some variant of our analysis may be relevant to the study of multimember proportional representation systems, an awareness of this fundamental assumption is essential.) We begin by introducing the following notation:

    c: the number of candidates for whom the citizen can vote,

    v: the number of voters in a particular election,

    n_k: the number of citizens voting for candidate k,

[2] *Ibid*, 38–39.

$(n_1, n_2, \ldots, n_c)$: an outcome of the election such that $\Sigma n_i = v$ if the citizen abstains and equals $v + 1$ if the citizen votes,

Ω: the set of possible outcomes if the citizen abstains, where the elements of this set are $(n_1, n_2, \ldots, n_c)$, with $\Sigma n_i = v$, and all $n_i \geq 0$,

Ω^1: the set of all possible outcomes if the citizen votes for candidate 1, where the elements of this set are $(n_1, n_2, \ldots, n_c)$, with $n_i \geq 0$, $n_1 \geq 1$, and $\Sigma n_i = v + 1$.[3]

$U(n_1, n_2, \ldots, n_c)$: the utility the citizen associates with an outcome $(n_1, n_2, \ldots, n_c) \in \Omega$,

$U^1(n_1, n_2, \ldots, n_c)$: the utility the citizen associates with an outcome $(n_1, n_2, \ldots, n_c) \in \Omega^1$,

$P(n_1, n_2, \ldots, n_c)$: the probability that outcome $(n_1, n_2, \ldots, n_c)$ occurs if the citizen does not vote,

$P^1(n_1, n_2, \ldots, n_c)$: the probability that outcome $(n_1, n_2, \ldots, n_c)$ occurs if the citizen votes for candidate 1.

The citizen now has $c + 1$ alternatives: vote for candidate 1, vote for candidate 2, and so on, or abstain. We assume that the efficacy of an alternative for realizing certain outcomes (members of the set Ω or Ω^1) determines the alternative's attractiveness. (Later we classify outcomes according to who wins or ties; here outcomes are differentiated by the number of votes each candidate receives.) To explore the functional correspondence between actions and outcomes, we observe that, in general, outcomes occur probabilistically; and we assume that these probabilities are functions of a citizen's actions. Hence, we construct the notational definition that the probability of a particular outcome $(n_1, n_2, \ldots, n_c)$ is $P(n_1, n_2, \ldots, n_c)$ if the citizen abstains, and that the probability of this outcome is $P^1(n_1, n_2, \ldots, n_c)$ if the citizen votes for candidate 1. Similarly, if A is a particular class of events in Ω (written $A \subset \Omega$), then $P(A)$ denotes the probability that A occurs if the citizen abstains. And if $A \subset \Omega^1$, $P^1(A)$ denotes the probability that A occurs if the citizen votes for candidate 1.[4] We assume, finally, that the citizen has a utility for each

---

[3] Formally,

$$\Omega = \{(n_1, \ldots, n_c) \mid \sum_{i=1}^{c} n_i = v, \, n_i \geq 0 \text{ for all } i\}$$

and

$$\Omega^1 = \{(n_1, \ldots, n_c) \mid \sum_{i=1}^{c} n_i = v + 1, \, n_1 \geq 1, \, n_i \geq 0 \text{ for all } i > 1\}.$$

[4] Because we are concerned here with the calculus of a single citizen, we assume that P and P^1 are subjective probabilities. These subjective probabilities, then, are functions of numerous factors, such as objective circumstances, access to polls, interest in the election, and education.

outcome in Ω and Ω^1. Symbolically, let $U(n_1, n_2, \ldots, n_c)$ be the utility of $(n_1, n_2, \ldots, n_c) \in \Omega$, and $U^1(n_1, n_2, \ldots, n_c)$ that of $(n_1, n_2, \ldots, n_c) \in \Omega^{1.5}$

These assumptions and definitions are sufficient for representing the expected utility the citizen derives from voting for candidate 1. If the citizen votes for candidate 1, each outcome $(n_1, n_2, \ldots, n_c) \in \Omega^1$ occurs with probability $P^1(n_1, n_2, \ldots, n_c)$, so the citizen receives the utility $U^1(n_1, n_2, \ldots, n_c)$ with the probability $P^1(n_1, n_2, \ldots, n_c)$. We express the expected utility of voting for candidate 1, E^1, as

$$(2) \qquad E^1 = \sum_{\Omega^1} P^1(n_1, n_2, \ldots, n_c) U^1(n_1, n_2, \ldots, n_c),$$

where the summation is taken over all $(n_1, n_2, \ldots, n_c) \in \Omega^1$.

We wish to compare this expected utility with the utility of abstaining; so we write the general expression for the expected utility of abstaining, E°, as

$$(3) \qquad E^\circ = \sum_{\Omega} P(n_1, n_2, \ldots, n_c) U(n_1, n_2, \ldots, n_c).$$

The citizen, therefore, prefers to vote for candidate 1 rather than to abstain if and only if $E^1 > E^\circ$, or equivalently, if and only if $E^1 - E^\circ > 0$.

To express this difference conveniently, however, we require an important additional assumption concerning the citizen's utility function. Observe that expressions (2) and (3) both involve a summation but that these summations are taken over different sets, Ω and Ω^1. Each set, however, can be partitioned into subsets of special significance. Specifically, we can identify first the subset of outcomes in which candidate 1 receives a plurality, and we can identify such a subset for each candidate. Second, we can identify the subsets of outcomes representing a particular first-place tie between two or more candidates, until all such ties are accounted for. We represent this delineation of the outcome subsets by introducing the following notation:

$\alpha = \{\alpha_1, \alpha_2, \ldots \alpha_m\}$: a set of integers with $1 \leq m \leq c$; $1 \leq \alpha_i \leq c$, $i = 1, 2, \ldots, m$, and $\alpha_i = \alpha_j$ if and only if $i = j$,

W_α: the set of outcomes $\{(n_1, n_2, \ldots, n_c)\} \subset \Omega$ such that $n_i = n_j$ if i and j are both equal to some integer in α, and $n_i > n_j$ if $i \in \alpha$ but $j \notin \alpha$,

$W_\alpha{}^1$: the same as above except that $\{(n_1, n_2, \ldots, n_c)\} \subset \Omega^1$.

---

[5] At this point we could introduce the cost of voting, C, and the utility the citizen derives from his sense of citizen duty, D, by adding D and $-C$ to $U^1(n_1, n_2, \ldots, n_c)$. The inclusion of D and C is, however, unnecessary, since they do not affect in any way an analysis without them; they are simply carried along unchanged in the analysis.

Thus, we employ α to identify certain outcomes so that, for example, $\alpha = \{2\}$ identifies the outcome "candidate 2 wins" and $\alpha = \{2, 3\}$ identifies the outcome "candidates 2 and 3 tie for first place." W_α is the set of all outcomes such that those candidates identified by α tie for first place if the citizen abstains, and $W_\alpha{}^1$ is a similar set in which the citizen votes for candidate 1.[6] We note also that $W_{\alpha'}$ and $W_{\alpha''}$ are disjoint sets if $\alpha' \neq \alpha''$; furthermore, the set of all W_α exhausts Ω.[7] (Similarly, $W_{\alpha'}{}^1$ and $W_{\alpha''}{}^1$ are disjoint if $\alpha' \neq \alpha''$, and the set of all $W_\alpha{}^1$ exhausts Ω^1.) Finally, the probability that the outcome W_α occurs is $P(W_\alpha)$, and the probability that $W_\alpha{}^1$ occurs is $P_\alpha{}^1(W_\alpha{}^1)$.

With this notation and delineation of outcomes we state our assumption.

Assumption 1: $U(n_1, n_2, \ldots, n_c) = U_\alpha$ for all $(n_1, n_2, \ldots, n_c) \in W_\alpha$, and $U^1(n_1, n_2, \ldots, n_c) = U_\alpha$ for all $(n_1, n_2, \ldots, n_c) \in W_\alpha{}^1$,

where U_α is some constant utility number greater than or equal to zero. Assumption 1 asserts, for example, that the citizen does not place more value on a landslide victory for his preferred candidate than on a victory with a bare plurality.[8] Assuming there are three candidates and ten voters, then the citizen derives the same utility U_1 from the outcomes $(5, 4, 1)$, $(5, 3, 2)$, $(5, 2, 3)$, $(6, 1, 2)$, and so on, i.e., all outcomes in which candidate 1 wins, and if he votes for candidate 1, he receives U_1 from the outcomes $(6, 4, 1)$, and so on.

Assumption 1 permits us to reexpress equations (2) and (3), therefore, as

$$[6]\ W_\alpha = \{(n_1, \ldots, n_c) \mid \sum_{i=1}^{c} n_i = v,\ n_{\alpha_j} = n_{\alpha_m}\ \text{if}\ \alpha_j,\ \alpha_m \in \alpha,\ \text{and}\ n_{\alpha_j} > n_{\alpha_m}\ \text{if}$$

$$\alpha_j \in \alpha,\ \alpha_m \notin \alpha\}$$

and

$$W_\alpha{}^1 = \{(n_1, \ldots, n_c) \mid \sum_{i=1}^{c} n_i = v + 1,\ n_{\alpha_j} = n_{\alpha_m}\ \text{if}\ \alpha_j,\ \alpha_m \in \alpha,\ \text{and}\ n_{\alpha_j} > n_{\alpha_m}\ \text{if}$$

$$\alpha_j \in \alpha,\ \alpha_m \notin \alpha\}.$$

Note that α is a set but we use it as a subscript also. This is done for notational convenience, where α becomes a list of integers when employed as a subscript.

[7] By disjoint we mean that $W_{\alpha'} \cap W_{\alpha'}{}^1 = \varnothing$, the empty set, if and only if $\alpha' \neq \alpha''$. Stated differently, an outcome $(n_1, \ldots, n_c)$ cannot represent both a two-way tie for first place between, say, candidates i and j, and a two-way tie for first place between some other combination of candidates. By exhausting Ω we mean that $\bigcup_\alpha W_\alpha = \Omega$.

[8] Assumption 1 is identical to the one implicitly made in the Riker and Ordeshook analysis. In their appendix, however, they consider continuous utility functions defined over the continuous approximation to Ω. See *op. cit.*, pp. 40–42.

(4) $$E^1 = \sum_\alpha P^1(W_\alpha{}^1)U_\alpha$$

and

(5) $$E^\circ = \sum_\alpha P(W_\alpha)U_\alpha,$$

where the summations are taken over all α. Thus we represent the difference $E^1 - E^\circ$ as

(6) $$E^1 - E^\circ = \sum_\alpha [P^1(W_\alpha{}^1) - P(W_\alpha)]U_\alpha.$$

Analysis of the term $[P^1(W_\alpha{}^1) - P(W_\alpha)]$ constitutes the core of this essay. To conduct such an analysis, however, we require an additional assumption.

Assumption 2: $P(n_1, n_2, \ldots, n_c) = P^1(n_1 + 1, n_2, \ldots, n_c)$.

Stated differently, the votes of other members of the electorate are unaffected when one person chooses to vote rather than abstain.[9] We postpone a detailed interpretation of Assumption 2 because this interpretation differs somewhat when considering two-candidate contests rather than multicandidate contests.

Expression (6), nevertheless, obviously conveys little substantive meaning. To ascertain the implications of this expression for a theory of voting, and to correct an error in the original analysis of equation (1), we consider, first, two-candidate contests.

2. Two-Candidate Contests

The error we must correct concerns the possibility of ties in elections. Riker and Ordeshook, in Table 2 of their article, assume that candidates 1 and 2 cannot tie.[10] Thus, using their notation, q' is the probability that candidate 1 wins if the citizen abstains and $1 - q'$ is the probability that candidate 2 wins. The probability of a tie, then, equals zero. They conclude, nevertheless, that P is greater than zero and that it equals the probability that the citizen's vote breaks a tie — which is obviously incon-

---

[9] This is the multicandidate equivalent of Assumption (18) and Lemma (19) presented in *ibid*, p. 30.
[10] *Ibid*, p. 29.

sistent with their initial assumption.[11] Since expression (6) allows ties we use it to deduce a correct expression for P.

First, if $c = 2$, the outcome sets Ω and Ω^1 are

$$\Omega = \{(n_1, n_2)| n_1 + n_2 = v, \text{ and } n_1, n_2 \geq 0\}$$
$$\Omega^1 = \{(n_1, n_2)| n_1 + n_2 = v + 1, \text{ and } n_1, n_2 \geq 0\}.$$

Thus, expressions (2) and (3) become

$$E^1 = \sum_{\alpha^1} P^1(n_1, n_2) U^1(n_1, n_2)$$

$$E^\circ = \sum_{\alpha} P(n_1, n_2) U(n_1, n_2).$$

Additionally, there are three admissible representations for α,

$$\alpha = \begin{cases} \{1\}: \text{ candidate 1 wins,} \\ \{2\}: \text{ candidate 2 wins,} \\ \{1, 2\}: \text{ candidates 1 and 2 tie.} \end{cases}$$

The partition subsets of Ω, then, are W_1, W_2, and W_{12}—the sets of outcomes in which candidate 1 wins, candidate 2 wins, and candidates 1 and 2 tie if the citizen does not vote. The partition subsets of Ω^1 are W_1^1, W_2^1, and W_{12}^1. Finally, from Assumption 1,

$$(7) \qquad U(n_1, n_2) = \begin{cases} U_1 \text{ if } n_1 > n_2 \text{ (i.e., } (n_1, n_2) \in W_1), \\ U_2 \text{ if } n_1 < n_2 \text{ (i.e., } (n_1, n_2) \in W_2), \\ U_{12} \text{ if } n_1 = n_2 \text{ (i.e., } (n_1, n_2) \in W_{12}). \end{cases}$$

An equivalent set of identities can be written for $U^1(n_1, n_2)$. We can now restate expressions (4) and (5) as

$$E^1 = P^1(W_1^1)U_1 + P^1(W_2^1)U_2 + P(W_{12}^1)U_{12}$$
$$E^\circ = P(W_1)U_1 + P(W_2)U_2 + P(W_{12})U_{12}.$$

Before we present the two-candidate equivalent of expression (6), however, it is convenient to introduce simpler notation. Let

$$(8) \qquad\qquad q_\alpha^1 = P^1(W_\alpha^1)$$

and

$$(9) \qquad\qquad q_\alpha^\circ = P(W_\alpha).$$

Thus, if $c = 2$, expression (6) is

$$(10) \quad E^1 - E^\circ = (q_1^1 - q_1^\circ)U_1 + (q_2^1 - q_2^\circ)U_2 + (q_{12}^1 - q_{12}^\circ)U_{12}.$$

[11] *Ibid*, p. 31.

We can simplify this equation if we use the following identities:

(11) $$q_2{}^1 - q_2{}^0 = -q_{12}{}^1$$

and

(12) $$q_1{}^1 - q_1{}^0 = q_{12}{}^0.$$

Before we can perform the substitution, however, we must demonstrate that (11) and (12) are true. To do so we use Assumption 2, which states that

(13) $$P(n_1, n_2) = P^1(n_1 + 1, n_2).$$

Stated differently, if we assume that the citizen's decision affects no other citizen's decision, the probability that (n_1, n_2) is the outcome when the citizen abstains is identical to the probability that $(n_1 + 1, n_2)$ is the outcome when he votes for candidate 1. We now prove equations (11) and (12).

We begin our proof by demonstrating that an outcome (n_1, n_2) is a member of the set W_2 if and only if the outcome $(n_1 + 1, n_2)$ is a member of the union of two sets, $W_2{}^1$ and $W_{12}{}^1$. Symbolically, we wish first to prove

$$(n_1, n_2) \in W_2 \Leftrightarrow (n_1 + 1, n_2) \in W_2{}^1 \cup W_{12}{}^1.$$

Let (n_1, n_2) be the outcome if the citizen does not vote: then $(n_1 + 1, n_2)$ is the corresponding outcome if the citizen votes for candidate 1. If $(n_1, n_2) \in W_2$, then, by definition, $(n_1, n_2) \in \Omega$, and $n_2 > n_1$. Assume the citizen now votes for candidate 1: then $(n_1 + 1, n_2) \in \Omega^1$, and $n_2 + 1 > n_1 + 1$. This is true if and only if $(n_1 + 1, n_2) \in \Omega^1$ and either $n_2 > n_1 + 1$, or $n_2 = n_1 + 1$, since, if $n_2 < n_1 + 1$, $n_2 + 1 \leq n_1 + 1$, which contradicts our previous statement. So, from the definition of $W_2{}^1$ and $W_{12}{}^1$, the outcome $(n_1 + 1, n_2)$ is either in $W_2{}^1$ or in $W_{12}{}^1$. Symbolically, this is written $(n_1 + 1, n_2) \in W_2{}^1 \cup W_{12}{}^1$, which is what we initially set out to demonstrate.

Substituting this result into expression (13) we obtain

$$P(W_2) = P^1(W_2{}^1 \cup W_{12}{}^1).$$

But $W_2{}^1$ and $W_{12}{}^1$ are disjoint subsets of Ω^1; so

$$P(W_2) = P^1(W_2{}^1) + P^1(W_{12}{}^1).$$

Thus, in terms of our original notation,

$$q_2{}^0 = q_2{}^1 + q_{12}{}^1,$$

or

$$q_2{}^1 - q_2{}^0 = -q_{12}{}^1,$$

which is equation (11). To prove equation (12) note that

$$q_1{}^0 + q_2{}^0 + q_{12}{}^0 = 1$$

and

$$q_1{}^1 + q_2{}^1 + q_{12}{}^1 = 1,$$

since these are the probabilities associated with exhaustive and disjoint sets of outcomes. Hence

$$q_1{}^0 = 1 - q_2{}^0 - q_{12}{}^0$$

and

$$q_1{}^1 = 1 - q_2{}^1 - q_{12}{}^1.$$

Subtracting $q_1{}^0$ from $q_1{}^1$,

$$q_1{}^1 - q_1{}^0 = (q_2{}^0 - q_2{}^1) + (q_{12}{}^0 - q_{12}{}^1).$$

And, from (11),

$$q_1{}^1 - q_1{}^0 = q_{12}{}^0,$$

which is equation (12).

We can now substitute expressions (11) and (12) into equation (10). After some simple algebraic manipulation we obtain

(14) $\qquad E^1 - E^0 = q_{12}{}^1(U_{12} - U_2) + q_{12}{}^0(U_1 - U_{12}).$

Equation (14) lends itself readily to verbal interpretation. First, $q_{12}{}^1$ is the probability that the citizen *creates* a tie with his vote. Thus, if he votes he receives the utility U_{12} with probability $q_{12}{}^1$; but if he fails to vote, candidate 2 receives a plurality of one vote, and the citizen receives the utility U_2 with probability $q_{12}{}^1$. The first term in (14), therefore, is the probability that the citizen's vote is decisive for a tie times the incremental benefit of creating this tie. Similarly, the second term equals the probability of *breaking* a tie times the incremental benefit of a victory for candidate 1 over the benefit derived from a tie. Hence, each term represents the utility difference between a favorable and an adjacent but less favorable outcome times the probability that the citizen's vote is decisive for the favored outcome. (We note that this pattern in the terms constituting the expected utility calculus reoccurs when we investigate multicandidate contests.)

Note, however, that equation (14) is not simply the product of two terms, such as PB. To make this reduction we require one additional assumption which is implicit in the Riker and Ordeshook analysis, but not explicitly identified as such. Specifically, let,

$$(15) \qquad\qquad U_{12} = \frac{U_1 + U_2}{2},$$

which is equivalent to the assumption that, if a tie occurs, the citizen is as likely to receive U_1, as U_2 (i.e., a fair coin is tossed to determine a winner). Substituting (15) into (14),

$$(16) \qquad E^1 - E^\circ = [q_{12}{}^1 + q_{12}{}^\circ]\left(\frac{U_1 - U_2}{2}\right).$$

Thus, in terms of the notation used to present the equation for the original calculus of voting, equation (1), P and B become respectively

$$(17) \qquad\qquad P = [q_{12}{}^1 + q_{12}{}^\circ]$$

and

$$(18) \qquad\qquad B = \frac{U_1 - U_2}{2}.$$

Riker and Ordeshook conclude that P is the probability that the citizen breaks a tie by voting, and that B is $(U_1 - U_2)$. We prove, however, that PB equals the probability of breaking a tie, $q_{12}{}^1$, *plus* the probability of creating a tie, $q_{12}{}^\circ$, times $(U_1 - U_2)/2$. Our reconstruction of the voting calculus, nevertheless, does not invalidate any of the substantive conclusions of Riker and Ordeshook, particularly their conclusion that P is a monotonic function of the closeness of a contest and not simply of the number of voters. B, similarly, remains a monotonic function of the utility differential between both candidates. (Note that we can arrive at an equivalent expression for PB if we assume that $q_{12}{}^1 = q_{12}{}^\circ$. This is a reasonable assumption since these are adjacent probabilities.[12] Hence, we obtain $E^1 - E^\circ = q_{12}{}^\circ(U_1 - U_2)$, which is the original formulation of PB.)

3. Three-Candidate Contests

Having corrected the original analysis of P we return to expression (6) and consider elections in which three candidates compete. First, we must

[12] By adjacent probabilities we mean that W_{12} occupies essentially the same position in Ω as does $W_{12}{}^1$ in Ω^1.

ascertain the candidate for whom the citizen votes if he does not abstain. If $U_1 > U_2 > U_3$, note that the possibility is not precluded that the expected value of voting for candidate 2 exceeds the expected utility of voting for candidate 1. Observe that if $c = 3$, there are seven possible configurations for α:

$$
\alpha = \begin{cases}
\{1\}: \text{candidate 1 wins,} \\
\{2\}: \text{candidate 2 wins,} \\
\{3\}: \text{candidate 3 wins,} \\
\{1, 2\}: \text{candidates 1 and 2 tie for first place,} \\
\{1, 3\}: \text{candidates 1 and 3 tie for first place,} \\
\{2, 3\}: \text{candidates 2 and 3 tie for first place, or} \\
\{1, 2, 3\}: \text{candidates 1, 2, and 3 tie.}
\end{cases}
$$

Thus, from the method used to develop equation (6), and from the notation introduced by (8), $E^1 - E^2$ is

$$
(19) \quad E^1 - E^2 = (q_1{}^1 - q_1{}^2)U_1 + (q_3{}^1 - q_3{}^2)U_2 + (q_{12}{}^1 - q_{12}{}^2)U_{12} \\
+ (q_{13}{}^1 - q_{13}{}^2)U_{13} + (q_{23}{}^1 - q_{23}{}^2)U_{23} + (q_{123}{}^1 - q_{123}{}^2)U_{123}.
$$

To show that $E^1 - E^2$, the expected utility of voting for candidate 1 minus the expected utility of voting for candidate 2, can be negative although $U_1 > U_2 > U_3$, assume that candidate 1 has little or no chance of winning or tying for first place. Thus, let

$$
(q_1{}^1 - q_1{}^2) = 0,
$$
$$
(q_{12}{}^1 - q_{12}{}^2) = 0,
$$
$$
(q_{13}{}^1 - q_{13}{}^2) = 0,
$$
$$
(q_{123}{}^1 - q_{123}{}^2) = 0,
$$

so that (19) becomes

$$
E^1 - E^2 = (q_2{}^1 - q_2{}^2)U_2 + (q_3{}^1 - q_3{}^2)U_3 + (q_{23}{}^1 - q_{23}{}^2)U_{23}.
$$

We adopt the usual convention that all utility numbers are greater than or equal to zero, so that $U_2 \geq U_3 \geq 0$, $U_{23} \geq 0$. But $(q_2{}^1 - q_2{}^2)$, $(q_3{}^1 - q_3{}^2)$, and $(q_{23}{}^1 - q_{23}{}^2)$ are each less than zero (e.g., the probability that candidate 2 wins if the citizen votes for 1, $q_2{}^1$, is obviously less than the probability that candidate 2 wins if the citizen votes for 2, $q_2{}^2$). $E_1 - E_2$, therefore, is a negative number; the citizen prefers to vote for candidate 2, his second choice. This is not an unanticipated result since it corroborates the advice that citizens should not vote for minor-party candidates when these candidates have little or no chance of winning or tying but should vote for viable candidates.

This conclusion forces us to supply an additional interpretation for Assumption 2. From the analysis of equation (19) we know that the citizen's revealed preference is a function of choices made by other citizens. Conversely, one would expect that the choices of others are affected by the citizen's decision. If only two candidates compete, variations in a candidate's viability affect turnout but not revealed preferences; citizens always vote for their preferred candidate if they vote. If more than two candidates compete, however, the citizen's decision to vote for candidate 1 rather than to abstain or to vote for another candidate affects, however slightly, the viability of candidates. This could affect the revealed preferences of other voters. But Assumption 2, when applied to multicandidate contests, precludes any possibility of the citizen's decision affecting either the turnout or the revealed preferences of others. We exclude, therefore, the dynamic interaction of citizens' actions, although in Section 6 we explore some dimensions of this problem.

With this interpretation of Assumption 2 we assume, without loss of generality, that if the citizen votes he votes for candidate 1 (while admitting the possibility that $U_2 > U_1$). For the case of three candidates expression (6) becomes

$$(20) \quad E^1 - E^\circ = (q_1{}^1 - q_1{}^\circ)U_1 + (q_2{}^1 - q_2{}^\circ)U_2 + (q_3{}^1 - q_3{}^\circ)U_3$$
$$+ (q_{12}{}^1 - q_{12}{}^\circ)U_{12} + (q_{13}{}^1 - q_{13}{}^\circ)U_{13} + (q_{23}{}^1 - q_{23}{}^\circ)U_{23}$$
$$+ (q_{123}{}^1 - q_{123}{}^\circ)U_{123}.$$

We now state, without proof, four identities that parallel expressions (11) and (12):

$$(21) \qquad\qquad q_1{}^1 - q_1{}^\circ = q_{123}{}^\circ + q_{12}{}^\circ + q_{13}{}^\circ,$$
$$(22) \qquad\qquad q_2{}^1 - q_2{}^\circ = -q_{12}{}^1,$$
$$(23) \qquad\qquad q_3{}^1 - q_3{}^\circ = -q_{13}{}^1,$$
$$(24) \qquad\qquad q_{23}{}^1 - q_{23}{}^\circ = -q_{123}{}^1.$$

The validity of these identities follows from Lemmas 1 and 2, which we present in Section 4; we indicate here their logical character. Consider, for example, expression (21). The subtraction $q_1{}^1 - q_1{}^\circ$ is the difference between the probability that candidate 1 wins if the citizen votes for 1 and the probability that candidate 1 wins if the citizen does not vote. Observe, however, that a citizen's vote is decisive if and only if candidate 1 ties for first place otherwise. The probabilities that such ties occur are $q_{123}{}^\circ$, $q_{12}{}^\circ$, and $q_{13}{}^\circ$. Hence, the citizen's increment to candidate 1's chances equals the probability that a single vote breaks any first-place tie involving candidate 1, which is exactly the implication of equation (21).

Expressions (22) and (23) are similar to expression (11), but instead of a single identity we now have two: the addition of a third candidate forces us to consider the possibility that candidates 1 and 3 tie for first place. No parallel expression exists, however, for equation (24) if only two candidates compete. The addition of a third candidate forces us to consider the possibility that a first-place tie occurs between the two candidates for whom the citizen does not vote.

Substituting equations (21) through (24) into equation (20) with some simple algebraic manipulation, we find that

$$(25) \quad E^1 - E^\circ = q_{123}{}^\circ(U_1 - U_{123}) + q_{12}{}^\circ(U_1 - U_{12}) + q_{13}{}^\circ(U_1 - U_{13})$$
$$+ q_{12}{}^1(U_{12} - U_2) + q_{13}{}^1(U_{13} - U_3) + q_{123}{}^1(U_{123} - U_{23}).$$

Equation (25) parallels equation (15); so we supply a parallel interpretation of the terms in (25). First, $q_{123}{}^\circ$ is the probability that the citizen breaks a three-way tie by voting. Thus, if he votes he receives the utility U_1 with probability $q_{123}{}^\circ$. But if he abstains, all three candidates tie with probability $q_{123}{}^\circ$; so he receives U_{123} with this probability. The first term, therefore, is the differential benefit of breaking a three-way tie times the probability of this event. Similarly, the second term is the differential benefit of breaking a two-way tie for first place between candidates 1 and 2 times the probability of this event, and so on.

Equation (25) is simplified now if we assume that

$$(26) \quad \begin{aligned} U_{123} &= \frac{U_1 + U_2 + U_3}{3}, \\ U_{12} &= \frac{U_1 + U_2}{2}, \\ U_{13} &= \frac{U_1 + U_3}{2}, \\ U_{23} &= \frac{U_2 + U_3}{2}, \end{aligned}$$

which is equivalent to the previous assumption for two-candidate contests (equation 16). Substituting (26) into (25),

$$(27) \quad E_1 - E^\circ = [q_{12}{}^1 + q_{12}{}^\circ]\frac{(U_1 - U_2)}{2} + [q_{13}{}^1 + q_{13}{}^\circ]\left(\frac{U_1 - U_3}{2}\right)$$
$$+ \left[q_{123}{}^\circ + \frac{q_{123}{}^1}{2}\right]\left(\frac{2U_1 - U_2 - U_3}{3}\right).$$

Rearranging terms,

$$(28) \quad E^1 - E = \left(\frac{U_1 - U_2}{2}\right)[q_{12}{}^1 + q_{12}{}^\circ + q_{123}{}^\circ/3 + q_{123}{}^1/6]$$
$$+ \left(\frac{U_1 - U_3}{2}\right)[q_{13}{}^1 + q_{13}{}^\circ + q_{123}{}^\circ/3 + q_{123}{}^1/6].$$

Observe now that the probabilities in the first term of (28) all concern the probabilities that candidates 1 and 2 are involved in first-place ties.

Similarly, the probabilities in the second term concern the probabilities that candidates 1 and 3 are involved in first-place ties. Thus, we have expressed $E^1 - E^\circ$ as a series of PB terms, where each of these terms represents the product of a utility difference times a measure of the relative competitiveness of the two candidates being compared.

To demonstrate more clearly these paired comparisons, assume that three-way ties are unlikely. Thus, for (28) we get

$$(29) \quad E^1 - E^\circ = \left(\frac{U_1 - U_2}{2}\right)(q_{12}{}^1 + q_{12}{}^\circ) + \left(\frac{U_1 - U_3}{2}\right)(q_{13}{}^1 + q_{13}{}^\circ),$$

which can now be seen as a simple extension of expression (16).

A geometric interpretation of our analysis is possible. We can represent (for three candidates) the sets of outcomes Ω and Ω^1 by a barycentric coordinate system — a triangle whose sides are the axes. We illustrate our analysis of three-candidate contests and the outcome set Ω for nine voters in Figure 2.1. The intersection of the *horizontal* lines with the points on the *left* side of the triangle indicates the number of citizens who vote for candidate 1. The intersection of the lines which slope *upward* from left to right with the points on the *right* side of the triangle indicates

Figure 2.1.   Outcome set Ω

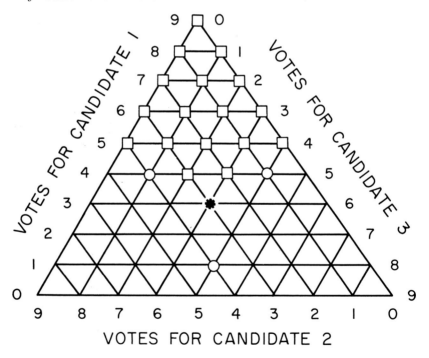

the number of citizens who vote for candidate 3. The intersection of the lines which slope *downward* from left to right with the points on the *base* of the triangle indicates the number of citizens who vote for candidate 2. Both the points on the sides and base of the triangle and the points within it represent the possible outcomes of the election if the citizen abstains. The crossed point in Figure 2.1, for example, represents the three-way tie (3, 3, 3), and the circled points (4, 4, 1), (4, 1, 4), and (1, 4, 4) represent the two-way ties for first place.

Observe that the point representing a three-way tie is located at the center of the triangle, whereas the points representing two-way ties for first place are located symmetrically about the center. (Of course, if v is not a multiple of three there is no point at the center of such a coordinate system; three-way ties cannot occur).

Interpreting our analysis now in terms of Figure 2.1, assume that this figure represents the election if the citizen does not vote. The points in Figure 2.1 with squares about them represent those outcomes in which candidate 1 is in undisputed possession of first place (i.e., the set W_1), and the probability that a squared point represents the outcome of the election is $q_1^\circ = P(W_1)$—the probability that candidate 1 wins if the citizen does not vote. If the citizen votes for candidate 1, Assumption 2 requires that we increase only the numbers on the axis indicating votes for candidate 1 by an increment of 1. The resulting outcome set Ω^1 is illustrated in Figure 2.2.

As in Figure 2.1, we circle points in Figure 2.2 representing two-way ties for first place; we place squares about points that represent an unambiguous victory for candidate 1. (Observe, however, that no point is crossed; no point can represent a three-way tie since the number of voters, 10, is not a multiple of three.) The probability that a squared point represents the outcome of the election is now q_1^1, the probability that candidate 1 wins if the citizen votes.

Using Figures 2.1 and 2.2 we can now illustrate expression (21), which states that $q_1^1 - q_1^\circ = q_{123}^\circ + q_{12}^\circ + q_{13}^\circ$. There are 17 outcomes in Figure 2.1 that signify a victory for candidate 1, but in Figure 2.2 there are 20 such points. If we superimpose these figures we learn that the additional three points in Figure 2.2 are exactly those points in Figure 2.1 representing a three-way tie, a two-way tie for first place between candidates 1 and 2, and a two-way tie for first place between candidates 1 and 3. And the probabilities that these points represent the outcome of the election are q_{123}°, q_{12}°, and q_{13}° respectively. Thus, $q_1^1 - q_1^\circ = q_{123}^\circ + q_{12}^\circ + q_{13}^\circ$, equation (21).

We shall not consider equations (22) through (24), but we can apply an equivalent procedure for illustrating their geometric properties. Such

Figure 2.2.   Outcome set Ω^1

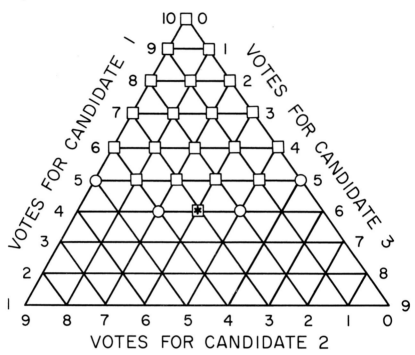

illustrations, nevertheless, do not prove the validity of these equations, which must follow logically from our premises. To do so we turn now to our general multicandidate model.

4. The General Multicandidate Model

We present in this section a general theory which extends the results presented in Sections 2 and 3 to elections with any number of candidates. (The proofs pertaining to this theory constitute Appendix I.) First, we present two lemmas which are the multicandidate generalizations of equations (21) through (24). Assuming now that the citizen either votes for candidate k or abstains, let $q_\alpha^{\ k}$, $W_\alpha^{\ k}$, and so on be the logical extensions of the notation introduced in Section 1. The first lemma, then, is

Lemma 1: For all α with $k \not\subset \alpha$, $q_\alpha^{\ \circ} = q_\alpha^{\ k} + q_{\alpha'}^{\ k}$,

in which α is the set of integers defined in Section 2 such that α does not contain k, and k is any integer ($1 \leq k \leq c$), and α' is the set of integers

α plus the integer k (symbolically, $\alpha' = \alpha \cup \{k\}$). Interpreting Lemma 1, if we let $k = 1$, $c = 3$, and $\alpha = 2$, the lemma states that $q_2^{\,\circ} = q_{\alpha'} + q_{12}^{\,1}$, or, equivalently, $q_2^{\,1} - q_2^{\,\circ} = q_{12}^{\,\circ}$. This is precisely expression (22). Consider a second example: let $\alpha = 2$, $c = 3$ and $k = 1$. Thus, the lemma asserts that $q_{23}^{\,\circ} = q_{23}^{\,1} + q_{123}^{\,1}$, or, equivalently, $q_{23}^{\,1} - q_{23}^{\,\circ} = -q_{123}^{\,1}$, which is expression (24).

The second lemma is

Lemma 2: $$q_k^{\,k} - q_k^{\,\circ} = \sum_{k \not\in \alpha} q_{\alpha'}^{\,\circ},$$

in which the summation is taken over all permissible configurations of α not containing k. Thus, if $k = 1$ and $c = 3$, these permissible configurations are $\{2\}$, and $\{3\}$, and $\{2, 3\}$. For $k = 1$ and $c = 3$, we obtain $q_1^{\,1} - q_1^{\,\circ} = q_{12}^{\,\circ} + q_{13}^{\,\circ} + q_{123}^{\,\circ}$, which is identical to expression (21). Expressions (21) through (24), therefore, are special cases of Lemmas 1 and 2. Similarly, expressions (11) and (12) are special cases of these two lemmas.

To state our general theorem let $\|\alpha\|$ be the number of integers comprising α, and make

Assumption 3: $$U_\alpha = \frac{\sum\limits_{i \in \alpha} U_i}{\|\alpha\|}.$$

This assumption states that the utility of a tie is the average of the utilities associated with the candidates involved in the tie. Thus, (30) is equivalent to equation (15) for two candidates, and to equation (26) for three candidates. We present the general expression for the expected utility of voting for candidate k minus the expected utility of abstaining in the following theorem.

Theorem: Under assumptions 1, 2, and 3

$$E^k - E^\circ = \sum_{k \not\in \alpha} \left(q_{\alpha'}^{\,\circ} + \frac{q_{\alpha'}^{\,k}}{\|\alpha\|} \right) \bar{U}_\alpha,$$

where

$$\bar{U}_\alpha = \frac{\sum\limits_{i \in \alpha} (U_k - U_i)}{\|\alpha'\|}.$$

Consider the statement of the theorem for $c = 3$. Let $k = 1$ so that the summation is taken over $\alpha = \{2\}$, $\{3\}$, and $\{2, 3\}$. First, we calculate $\bar{U}_\alpha$:

$$\overline{U}_2 = (U_1 - U_2)/2,$$
$$\overline{U}_3 = (U_1 - U_3)/2,$$
$$\overline{U}_{23} = ((U_1 - U_2) + (U_1 - U_3))/3 = (2U_1 - U_2 - U_3)/3.$$

Substituting these identities into the statement of the theorem,

$$E^k - E^\circ = (q_{12}{}^\circ + q_{12}{}^1)\frac{(U_1 - U_2)}{2} + (q_{13}{}^\circ + q_{13}{}^1)\frac{(U_1 - U_3)}{2}$$
$$+ \left(q_{123}{}^\circ + \frac{q_{123}{}^1}{2}\right)\left(\frac{2U_1 - U_2 - U_3}{3}\right),$$

which is identical to equation (27).

An immediate corollary of this theorem permits us to express $E^k - E^\circ$ as a series of summed terms involving only probabilities of two-way ties, plus a series of summed terms involving only probabilities of three-way ties, and so on.[13]

Corollary 1:

$$E^k - E^\circ = \sum_{i \neq k}(q_{ik}{}^\circ + q_{ik}{}^k)\left[\frac{U_k - U_i}{2}\right]$$
$$+ \sum_{i \neq j \neq k}\left(q_{ijk}{}^\circ + \frac{q_{ijk}{}^k}{2}\right)\left[\frac{2U_k - U_i - U_j}{3}\right]$$
$$+ \sum_{h \neq i \neq j \neq k}\left(q_{hijk}{}^\circ + \frac{q_{hijk}{}^k}{3}\right)\left[\frac{3U_k - U_i - U_j - U_h}{4}\right]$$
$$+ \cdots.$$

For $c = 3$, Corollary 1 is simply a restatement of expression (27). This corollary does, however, emphasize the general pattern in the calculation of $E^k - E^\circ$, which may not be evident in our theorem. Observe now that by rearranging terms, the statement of Corollary 1 can be reexpressed as

Corollary 2:

$$E^k - E^\circ = \left[\frac{U_k - U_1}{2}\right](q_{1k}{}^\circ + q_{1k}{}^1 + q_{1jk}{}^\circ/3 + q_{1jk}{}^1/6 + q_{1ijk}{}^\circ/4$$
$$+ q_{1ijk}{}^1/12 + \cdots) + \left[\frac{U_k - U_2}{2}\right](q_{2k}{}^\circ + q_{2k}{}^1$$
$$+ q_{2jk}{}^\circ/3 + \cdots) + \left[\frac{U_k - U_3}{2}\right](\cdots) + \cdots.$$

[13] The notation $\Sigma_{i \neq j \neq k}$, for example, implies a double summation, of which there are ${}_nC_3$ terms, taken over all values of i and j from 1 to c such that $i \neq j \neq k$. Thus $\Sigma_{h \neq i \neq j \neq k}$ implies a triple summation of which there are ${}_nC_4$ terms, taken over all values of h, i, and j from 1 to c such that $h \neq i \neq j = k$.

Thus, the efficacy of voting, $E^k - E^\circ$, equals a series of utility comparisons between pairs of candidates times a probability, which for three candidates is represented by expression (27). Specifically, to calculate $E^k - E^\circ$ we compare candidate k with each of the remaining candidates by computing a utility difference and a sum of probabilities. Note that this sum involves all the ways in which the two candidates being compared can tie for first place. Thus we can take this sum as a measure of the competitiveness between the two relevant candidates. Stated differently, we can express $E^k - E^\circ$ as

$$(30) \qquad E^k - E^\circ = B^{k1}P^{k1} + B^{k2}P^{k2} + \cdots$$

Thus, we can express the efficacy of voting as a series of paired comparisons, in which each comparison involves a calculation of a utility difference and a measure of relative competitiveness.

We can further simplify expression (30) if we assume that

$$q_\alpha{}^k = q_\alpha{}^\circ$$

for all α and k (this is a restatement of the assumption that adjacent probabilities in comparable outcome spaces are equal) and if we supply an approximation which, stated as an assumption, is

Assumption 4: If $\|\alpha^1\| > \|\alpha^2\|$, then $q_\alpha{}^{j_1} \ll q_\alpha{}^{j_2}$, for all j.

Assumption 4 states that only two-way ties are likely. Thus, for $c = 3$ we let $q_{123}{}^\circ = q_{123}{}^1 = 0$. Employing these assumptions, we get from Corollary 1 or 2

$$E^k - E^\circ \cong \sum_{i \neq k} q_{ik}{}^\circ (U_k - U_i),$$

which is a simplified version of expression (30).

Before we conclude our general discussion we can deduce one result concerning the candidate for which the citizen prefers to vote. Recall from our previous discussion that citizens can choose rationally to vote for candidates who are not their first preferences. This possibility arises because a citizen's most preferred candidate may not be a viable alternative, in which case the citizen either abstains or votes for some more viable candidate. To ascertain which choice a citizen makes, we state a third corollary,

Corollary 3: A citizen votes for the candidate who maximizes $E^k - E^\circ$, but if no $E^k - E^\circ > 0$, the citizen abstains.

Clearly, the citizen prefers to vote for candidate k rather than candidate j if $E^k - E^\circ > E^j - E^\circ$. And if $E^k - E^\circ > E_j - E^\circ$ for all $j = 1$,

2, . . . , c $(j \neq k)$, he either votes for k or he abstains. Finally, if $E^k >$ $E°$, he prefers to vote for k rather than to abstain. Thus, the citizen selects the alternative that maximizes the expected utility of voting less the expected utility of abstaining.

We began our analysis by noting the lack of generality of the original voting calculus. We then reconstructed the logical foundations of this calculus so that we can analyze the decision to vote when the number of candidates exceeds two. The product of this reconstruction is Corollaries 1 and 2, and equation (30)—the multicandidate analogue of expression (1) without C and D. Our corollaries express generally the efficacy of voting for citizens who decide as if they are expected utility maximizers. The relative efficacy of voting for candidate k, $E^k - E°$, is a function (approximately) of a series of terms, each representing a paired comparison. The multicandidate generalization of PB, therefore is a series of terms in which each term represents a paired comparison between candidate k and some other candidate. The empirical implications of this result are:

1. A single subjective index of competitiveness is unsatisfactory. P's empirical referents are a series of subjective measures of competitiveness between candidate pairs.
2. A single subjective index of the election's importance is unsatisfactory. B's empirical referents are a set of paired utility comparisons.

Theory construction, nevertheless, should involve more than the simple algebraic extension of an earlier derivation. Ideally, new and valuable theories also provide nonobvious insights into phenomena that initially are not believed to be in its domain. So that we might analyze further the implications of our theory we proceed to Sections 5 and 6.

5. The 2- and 3-Candidate Contests Compared

It seems reasonable, with our theory, to contrast the efficacy of voting for alternative values of c. Specifically, we can study how the number of candidates affects the motivation to vote. Such an analysis is relevant to the comparative study of alternative electoral institutions if we expect the number of candidates to vary with the alternatives. Before we proceed, however, we must reiterate a note of caution: we assume throughout the development of our theory that the winner takes all. Hence, institutional comparisons derived from our theory must be carefully scrutinized—particularly with reference to proportional representation systems—to avoid violating this assumption. Because we contrast only contests with two candidates and contests with three candidates, it is safer to interpret our analysis as an examination of the turnout effect of a third candidate's entry into a two-candidate arena.

Our analysis begins with the observation that if two candidates compete with utilities $U_1 > U_2$, the efficacy of voting, $E^1 - E^\circ$, is $(q_{12}^\circ + q_{12}^1)$ $(U_1 - U_2)/2$. Let $\Pi_2 = E^1 - E^\circ$ and $P_{12} = (q_{12}^\circ + q_{12}^1)$ if $c = 2$. Thus,

$$\Pi_2 = P_{12}(U_1 - U_2)/2, \quad c = 2.$$

When a third candidate, with utility U_3, enters the contest, the citizen's efficacy for voting for candidate 1, say Π_3, becomes

$$\Pi_3 = P_{12}'(U_1 - U_2)/2 + P_{13}'(U_1 - U_3)/2, \quad c = 3,$$

where $P_{12}' = q_{12}^\circ + q_{12}^1$, $P_{13}' = q_{13}^\circ + q_{13}^1$, and the q^k's are now the probabilities of ties when the number of candidates equals 3. Note that although the notation used to represent the probabilities of ties in a two-candidate contest is the same as that used in three-candidate contests, there is no reason to suppose that these probabilities are equal. In fact, we show, for example, that $P_{12} \neq P_{12}'$ under the conditions we assume. Hence, we cannot infer without additional analysis anything about the relative magnitudes of Π_2 and Π_3.

To calculate and compare P_{12}, P_{12}', and P_{13}', we must make additional assumptions about the underlying probability density function that the citizen associates with the outcome spaces.

Assumption 5: if $c = 2$, $P(n_1, n_2) = P(n_1', n_2')$ for all (n_1, n_2), (n_1', n_2') $\in \Omega$, and if $c = 3$, $P(n_1, n_2, n_3) = P(n_1', n_2', n_3')$ for all (n_1, n_2, n_3), $(n_1', n_2', n_3') \in \Omega$.

An equivalent interpretation of Assumption 5 is that the citizen is totally uncertain about the probable outcome of an election; so he assumes that all outcomes are equiprobable. Stated differently, candidate 1 has as good a chance of securing no votes as 1, 2, . . . , v votes. Obviously, this is not an assumption which generally corresponds to reality, and even for use in a null model it is suspect. It is the only assumption, though, which thus far yields any manageable analysis, and so we adopt it.

With this assumption, we can easily show that $q_{12}^\circ = q_{13}^\circ$, $q_{12}^1 = q_{13}^1$ for $c = 3$; so $P_{12}' = P_{13}'$. Hence, we have the two equations

(31a)
$$\Pi_2 = P_{12}\left(\frac{U_1 - U_2}{2}\right)$$

and

(31b)
$$\Pi_3 = P_{12}'\left[\left(\frac{U_1 - U_2}{2}\right) + \left(\frac{U_1 - U_3}{2}\right)\right]$$
$$= P_{12}'\left[\frac{2U_1 - U_2 - U_3}{2}\right].$$

Equations (31a) and (31b) are not sufficient, however, for conducting a comparative analysis. We must ascertain the magnitude of both P_{12} and P_{12}'. We can compute P_{12} readily if $c = 2$. If there are v voters, there are $v + 1$ outcomes: candidate 1 receives 0, 1, 2, . . . , or v votes. From Assumption 5, these outcomes are equiprobable; so the probability of a tie existing, or of the citizen being able to create a tie, i.e., $(q_{12}{}^\circ + q_{12}{}^1)$, is simply $1/(v + 1)$.[14] Thus, from (31a),

$$(32) \qquad \Pi_2 = \frac{U_1 - U_2}{2(v + 1)} .$$

Computing P_{12}' for $c = 3$, however, is more difficult, so in Appendix II we prove, with Assumption 5, that

$$(33) \qquad P_{12}' = (q_{12}{}^1 - q_{12}{}^\circ) = \frac{2\left|\left[\dfrac{v + 2}{3}\right]\right|}{(v + 1)(v + 2)} .$$

($|[X]|$ reads "the greatest integer, say i, such that $i \leq X$." If $v = 8$, for example, $|[10/3]| = 3$, and $q{}^\circ_{13} = 1/15$.) Equation (31b) thus becomes

$$(34) \qquad \Pi_3 = \frac{(2U_1 - U_2 - U_3)\left|\left[\dfrac{v + 2}{3}\right]\right|}{(v + 1)(v + 2)} .$$

Equations (32) and (34) allow us to contrast the relative magnitudes of Π_2 and Π_3. Obviously, these magnitudes depend on v and the U's. We prove in Appendix II the following limit theorem in lieu of considering alternative values of these parameters.[15]

Theorem 2: With Assumption 5, as $v \to \infty$

$$\Pi_2 \geq \Pi_3 \Leftrightarrow U_1 - U_3 \leq U_3 - U_2 \Leftrightarrow \lambda = \frac{U_3 - U_2}{U_1 - U_2} > -\frac{1}{2}$$

and

$$\Pi_2 < \Pi_3 \Leftrightarrow U_1 - U_3 > U_3 - U_2 \Leftrightarrow \lambda = \frac{U_3 - U_2}{U_1 - U_2} < \frac{1}{2} .$$

---

[14] Note that this calculation for $q_{12}{}^\circ$ is identical to the calculation questioned by Riker and Ordeshook as a means for calculating P. They are correct in rejecting this value, however, only if Assumption 5 is not satisfied.

[15] It is readily confirmed that: if $v + 2$ is a multiple of 3, $\Pi_2 \geq \Pi_3$ if and only if $\lambda \geq \frac{1}{2}$, and $\Pi_2 < \Pi_3$ otherwise; if $v + 1$ is a multiple of 3, $\Pi_2 \geq \Pi_3$ if and only if $\lambda \geq \frac{1}{2}(v - 2)/(v + 1)$, and $\Pi_2 < \Pi_3$ otherwise, and; if v is a multiple of 3, $\Pi_2 \geq \Pi_3$ if and only if $\lambda \geq \frac{1}{2}(v - 6)/v$, and $\Pi_2 < \Pi_3$ otherwise. Observe that, for each case, Theorem 2 is satisfied as $v \to \infty$ (i.e., $\lim_{v \to \infty}(v - 2)/(v + 1) = 1$, and $\lim_{v \to \infty}(v - 6)/v = 1$).

Theorem 2 requires some interpretation. First, restating this theorem, if the utility the citizen derives from candidate 3 is closer to the utility he derives from the first candidate than from the second candidate (i.e., $\lambda \geq \frac{1}{2}$), the efficacy of voting for the first candidate is greatest in two-candidate contests. If, however, U_3 is closer to U_2 than to U_1 (i.e., $\lambda < \frac{1}{2}$), the efficacy of voting is greatest in three-candidate contests. Thus, the relative utility the citizen derives from a new candidate who enters a two-candidate contest determines whether or not the citizen's incentives for voting for his previously most preferred candidate increase. We conjecture, however, that the critical value of $\lambda - \frac{1}{2}$—is a consequence of Assumption 5. Stated differently, we conjecture that if some other prior probability density functions for outcomes are postulated, the critical value of λ would not necessarily equal $\frac{1}{2}$.

Theorem 2, nevertheless, serves as a counterexample to the assertion that, *ceteris paribus*, turnout in multicandidate contests necessarily exceeds turnout in two-candidate contests. This assertion generally assumes some variant of the abstention from alienation hypothesis, where citizens abstain if a satisfactory candidate is unavailable. Thus, turnout increases as candidates are added because the probability that at least one candidate satisfies some minimal standard increases. The central concerns of our analysis—indifference and the probability of altering outcomes—are frequently ignored in such comparisons, however, because the voting patterns of citizens who are largely satisfied are forgotten.

Specifically, consider the case where U_3 is not greater than both U_1 and U_2. Observe that if the citizen is indifferent between candidates 1 and 3 (i.e., if $U_1 = U_3 > U_2$ so that $\lambda = 1$), the addition of candidate 3 reduces the efficacy of voting. Thus, among citizens with this preference, turnout decreases when such a third candidate is added. Assumption 5 explains this result. If $U_1 = U_3 > U_2$, the citizen is unconcerned about breaking ties between candidates 1 and 3, so that the only relevant impact the citizen's vote has on the election is that of breaking a tie between candidates 1 and 2. But the implication of Assumption 5 is that the probability of such a tie is smaller if three candidates compete than if only two such candidates are available. Thus, $\Pi_2 > \Pi_3$.

The directional change of turnout derived from our analysis and from the alienation hypothesis correspond, however, if $U_1 > U_3 = U_2$. Here if three candidates compete the citizen is concerned about breaking either of two ties, whereas if only two candidates compete only one tie can be broken. Thus, $\Pi_3 > \Pi_2$.

We may state our conclusion somewhat imprecisely. First, the alienation hypothesis may account for variations in turnout among citizens who are unsatisfied initially with candidates 1 and 2 but who are satisfied with the new candidate. Second, for those citizens who are satisfied initially some variant of Theorem 2 may explain variations in their turnout as new candidates are added.

6. Turnout and Competition

We present in this section an analysis of equation (29), in which the degree of competition varies. Riker and Ordeshook conclude that PB is greatest when the most likely outcome is a tie. The logical extension of this conclusion for three candidates appears to be that $E^k - E^\circ$ is greatest if the most likely outcome is a three-way tie. We show, nevertheless,

Figure 2.3.   Barycentric coordinate system with v large

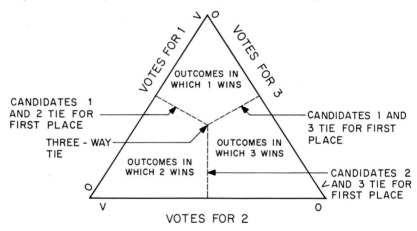

that some citizens' turnout is *not* greatest if the three candidates are identically matched in numerical strength; $E^k - E^\circ$ is greatest for citizens who prefer candidate k if candidate k is slightly ahead of his two opponents.

A rigorous proof of this assertion constitutes Appendix III; here we define geometrically the context of this proof. We illustrate in Figure 2.3 a barycentric coordinate system in which v, the number of voters, is large. Thus, instead of delineating outcomes by discrete points, we approximate the outcome space with continuous lines and areas.

We assume that the citizen behaves as if he estimates a probability density function, g, over this set of outcomes, such that g is the continuous equivalent of $P(n_1, n_2, n_3)$. We assume, also, that g is a circularly symmetric function (i.e., the constant probability contours of g are circles).[16] Paralleling the Riker and Ordeshook interpretation of the statement "the most likely outcome is a tie," we interpret geometrically the statement "the most likely outcome is a three-way tie" by assuming that the mean of g, μ, is the point representing a three-way tie. We illustrate the contours of g in Figure 2.4.

Assume now that the citizen prefers candidate 1, and consider our reduced form of expression (28) — expression (29). From the definitions of g and the lines L_1 and L_2 in Figure 2.4, we can see that the two probabilities q_{12}° and q_{13}° (or q_{12}^{1} and q_{13}^{1}) can be thought of generally as the

Figure 2.4. Contours of g

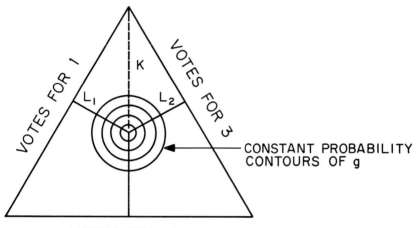

VOTES FOR 2

areas under g along L_1 and L_2. Thus, because U_1, U_2, and U_3 are constants, $E^1 - E^{\circ}$ is maximized when g is centered in the outcome space if and only if these areas also are maximized. We prove (in Appendix III), however, that this area is not maximized when g is centered in the outcome space. More formally, we define first the line K, which connects the center of the coordinate system to the vertex representing the maximum number of votes for candidate 1 — the upper vertex in Figure 2.4. Second, we denote the center of our coordinate system by 0. Note that as we proceed from 0, along K, to the upper vertex, candidate 1's vote increases at the expense of his two opponents. This increase is the result of equally

[16] If we imposed Assumption 5 (which we do not), the function g would be a uniform density. Instead, we assume now that the citizen believes that some outcomes are more likely than others. We let g be circularly symmetric, however, because, at this point in the development of our theory, there does not appear to be any reason to suppose that g assumes a nonsymmetric form.

numerous defections from both candidates 2 and 3 to candidate 1. Finally, we assume that the domain of g is bounded so that variations in μ along K are permissible.[17]

We prove the following result with these assumptions.

For μ on K and U_1, U_2, and U_3 constant, $E^1 - E^\circ$ is maximized for some unique $\mu \neq 0$.

Thus, $E^1 - E^\circ$ is maximized for a value of μ such that g is not centered at the point representing a three-way tie.

While this result might appear to be counterintuitive, inspection of both equation (29) and the effects of varying μ reveals that it should be anticipated. Consider the probabilities of ties occurring if the citizen abstains. Note that the probability of a tie between candidates 2 and 3, q_{23}°, does not enter (29); only ties between the preferred candidate and his opponents are relevant. Thus, if we increase q_{12}° and q_{13}° at the expense of q_{23}°, $E^1 - E^\circ$ increases. And this is precisely what we accomplish by increasing μ from 0 along K. (Of course, if μ is increased too much, all three probabilities decrease.)

We can interpret this result more readily if its implications are stated in dynamic terms. Assume: (1) that when the citizen believes that the election is closely contested, $\mu = 0$, and (2) that an increase in μ from 0 (along K) corresponds to the citizen's belief that candidate 1's fortunes are improving (at the expense of his opponents). Thus, variations in μ represent variations in the citizen's subjective estimate that candidate 1 wins. Stated somewhat imprecisely, our result asserts, therefore, that for citizens who prefer candidate 1: (1) the turnout increases as candidate 1 pulls ahead; (2) the turnout is greatest when candidate 1 achieves a slight advantage over his opponents, and (3) *ceteris paribus*, the turnout decreases thereafter. Moreover, we conjecture that increased turnout among citizens who prefer candidate 1 as μ increases is accompanied by decreased turnout among citizens who prefer candidates 2 and 3. We do not show this rigorously for small values of μ, although it is clear that this occurs for large values of μ.

This analysis suggests a partial explanation for bandwagon effects. Discussions about such effects commonly concern a shift in electoral support in favor of a candidate whose fortunes appear to be improving. One

---

[17] The total area under a probability density function must equal 1. The assumption that g is bounded permits us to vary μ while we keep both the area under g equal to 1 and its functional form unchanged. Riker and Ordeshook make a similar assumption in their appendix when they assumed that, in their notation, $g(x - x_0)$ goes to zero sufficiently rapidly. See *op. cit.*, p. 40.

explanation for these shifts is that some voters wish to be on the side of the winner, while political activists (e.g., party organizations and financial contributors) maximize postelectoral resources by supporting candidates likely to win. Undoubtedly, a sizable variation in voter and activist support derives from the reasonable desire to share the psychic and material rewards of supporting victorious candidates. An account of such incentives, however, is external to our analysis since the utility associated with a particular candidate is prohibited by Assumption 1 from being dependent on the citizen's actions. Only the probability of realizing this utility is a function of the citizen's acts.

Our analysis supplies a complementary hypothesis: bandwagons result from the behavior of voters and activists whose increased turnout and support derive from a desire to affect the outcome. Such increases are rational because a person's effect on the outcome is greatest when his preferred candidate is slightly ahead, and not when the contest is a three-way dead heat.

But even within the structure of our model, our analysis is clearly incomplete and possibly misleading since bandwagons might also come from shifts in revealed preferences for candidates. Specifically, as we demonstrate in the introduction to Section 3, voters switch to viable candidates as one candidate pulls ahead because of variations in the probability of realizing certain outcomes. If the leading candidate benefits most from such switching, a bandwagon effect is observed. We observe, however, that, from equation (19), if each citizen can be characterized by one of the following preference orderings, a citizen votes only for his preferred candidate (or abstains):

$$U_1 > U_2 = U_3,$$
$$U_2 > U_1 = U_3,$$
$$U_3 > U_1 = U_2.$$

Thus, with only these preference possibilities, bandwagons arise in our model only as a result of variations in turnout.

We cannot guarantee, of course, that these possibilities characterize the electorate. If they do not, our explanation is incomplete since both turnout and revealed preference are interdependent. Revealed preference affects the candidates' viabilities, which affect turnout, which again affects the candidates' viabilities, which affect revealed preference, and so on. Our subject here, however, is not the analysis of the dynamic case: we have not yet analyzed all ramifications of our theory for the initial assumptions. We hope that a dynamic analysis can be the focus of a future paper.

7. Conclusion

We began with a theory of the calculus of voting which is obviously inadequate for analyzing multicandidate elections. We reconstructed the logical foundations of this theory, and we deduced a general multicandidate expression for the expected utility of voting minus the expected utility of abstaining. We then examined the implications of this expression for the comparison of turnout in two- and three-candidate contests and for variations in the competitiveness of three-candidate contests. This examination revealed two nonobvious implications: (1) the addition of a third candidate to a two-candidate contest decreases the efficacy of voting for some citizens; hence, turnout does not increase necessarily, *ceteris paribus*, as additional candidates join an election contest; and (2) the efficacy of voting, for some citizens, increases as one candidate pulls slightly ahead of his two competitors. Turnout, therefore, is not necessarily greatest if the contest is a three-way dead heat.

Despite the derivation of these propositions, some readers may object to the complexities of our calculations, arguing that few if any citizens bother to analyze the effect of their vote in such detail. We cannot ignore the assertions, moreover, that some people cannot calculate expected utilities and cannot ascertain the logical consequences of their actions, or that they are simply stupid. Undoubtedly, these observations, if they are true, call for deviations from the model's predictions. We emphasize, however, that academic excellence or a facility with mathematics is not a prerequisite for rational action.[18] We postulate goals for people and infer a mathematical calculus from these goals, not because people really perform such calculations, but because they act *as if* they do. Milton Friedman constructs the enlightening example of the expert billiard player.[19] To explain and to predict such a player's actions, we infer that he employs the theorems of trigonometry and geometry. That the billiard player is not consciously familiar with such theorems and, if asked, replies that he chooses the way he shoots by experience and a "feel" for the game, does not constitute empirical evidence contrary to the inferred calculus. Thus, we assert that such a player calculates his shots *as if* he uses trigonometry and geometry. Hence, many people are unable to

---

[18] For an excellent treatment of the problem of error and rationality, see Arthur S. Goldberg, "Social Determinism and Rationality as Bases of Party Identification," *American Political Science Review*, LXIII (March, 1969), 5–25.

[19] Milton Friedman, "The Methodology of Positive Economics," *Essays in Positive Economics* (Chicago: University of Chicago Press, 1963), 3–43.

comprehend our descriptions of their actions, but we infer that these descriptions are correct to the extent that they satisfy the scientific canons of prediction and parsimonious explanation.

Citizens, however, are not analogous to expert billiard players because citizens may be relatively unconcerned about voting, whereas billiard players expend much effort learning their game. Our theory appears silly or superfluous, therefore, if our assumptions imply "expert" citizens. Citizens, individually, spend little time voting, and frequently their calculus includes no more than C and D: they vote if they are socialized to do so, and otherwise they abstain. We can argue, nevertheless, that *collectively* citizens have a great amount of available expertise, particularly when they obtain their cues about voting from polls, opinion leaders, and activists, who may indeed be "expert voters." Practice and physical coordination are necessary to perform well in billiards, even when expert instruction is available; but it is relatively easy to follow instructions about voting successfully. Thus, while most people cannot act like expert billiard players simply on the basis of verbal advice, a voter who takes his cues from opinion leaders and activists with whose goals he agrees can act like an expert voter. Hence, it is reasonable to believe that our assumptions are correct for citizens who are not consciously aware of our calculus. Of course, the only valid justification for our theory is empirical evidence. We hope that empirical research into electoral participation might subject our analysis to this ultimate test.

Appendix I

Proofs of Lemmas 1 and 2 and Theorem 1 from Section 4

LET R^c be the c-dimensional Euclidean vector space (e.g., a c-dimensional coordinate system where each axis is the real line) with elements $\bar{n} = (n_1, n_2, \cdots, n_c)$, and let $\Omega \subset R^c$ be defined as

$$\Omega = \{\bar{n} | \sum_{i=1}^{c} n_i = v, \text{ and each } n_i \text{ is a nonnegative integer}\}.$$

For any positive integer v_o, Ω represents the space of all possible outcomes in an electoral contest between c candidates with v_o voters, where outcomes are defined in terms of the number of votes each candidate receives.

Now suppose that $P(\bar{n})$ is a probability density function on Ω (i.e., Ω is the domain of $P(\bar{n})$). Therefore,

$$\sum_{\bar{n} \in \Omega} P(\bar{n}) = 1, \text{ and } P(\bar{n}) \geq 0 \text{ for all } \bar{n} \in \Omega.$$

Thus, we assume that $P(\bar{n})$ behaves like an objective probability density function. Also, if $A \subseteq \Omega$, we write

$$P(A) = \sum_{\bar{n} \in A} P(\bar{n}).$$

Suppose further that we have another real valued function on Ω, say $U(\bar{n})$. Then,

(1a) $$E^\circ = E(U) = \sum_{\bar{n} \in \Omega} P(\bar{n}) U(\bar{n})$$

is the expected value of U over Ω. For our purposes, $P(\bar{n})$ is the citizen's estimate of the probability of the occurrence of a specific outcome, $\bar{n}$, if he does not vote. Also, $U(\bar{n})$ is the utility that the citizen derives from the outcome $\bar{n}$. Hence, $E°$ is the citizen's expected utility of abstaining.

For each candidate k we now let $P^k(\bar{n})$ be the probability density function of Ω^k, and we let $U^k(\bar{n})$ be a real valued function of Ω^k. We set

$$(2a) \qquad E^k = E(U^k) = \sum_{\bar{n} \in \Omega} p_k{}^k(\bar{n})U^k(\bar{n})$$

where Ω^k is the set of all possible outcomes if the citizen votes for candidate k; $P^k(\bar{n})$ is the citizen's subjective probability estimate that a specific outcome occurs if he votes for candidate k, and $U^k(\bar{n})$ is the utility he derives from that outcome. $E^k - E°$ represents the expected utility of voting for candidate k minus the expected utility of abstaining.

We now make some assumptions about P, P^k, U, and U^k to simplify the calculation of $E^k - E°$. First, we consider the 2^c subsets of the form,

$$\alpha = \{\alpha_1, \alpha_2, \alpha_3, \cdots, \alpha_m\} \text{ with } 1 \le \alpha_j \le c \text{ for all } j; \alpha_j \text{ all integers};$$
$$1 \le m \le c, \text{ and } \alpha_j = \alpha_i \text{ if and only if } i = j.$$

Let

$$\Gamma = \{\alpha | \alpha \text{ is a set in the above form}\}.$$

For each $\alpha \in \Gamma$ such that $k \not\subset \alpha$, let $\alpha' = \alpha \cup \{k\}$. And for each $\alpha \in \Gamma$, let

$$W_\alpha = \{\bar{n} \mid \bar{n} \in \Omega, n_j = n_k \text{ for } k, j \in \alpha, \text{ and } n_j > n_k$$
$$\text{for } j \in \alpha, k \not\subset \alpha\}$$

and

$$W_\alpha{}^k = \{\bar{n} \mid \bar{n} \in \Omega^k, n_j = n_k \text{ for } k, j \in \alpha, \text{ and } n_j > n_k$$
$$\text{for } j \in \alpha, k \not\subset \alpha\}.$$

Observe that each set α corresponds to some subset of the c candidates, and that W_α is the set of all outcomes where this set of candidates wins. (If there is more than one candidate in the set, α is the set of candidates who tie for first place). Thus, if α consists of a single element, say k, then W_α is the set of all outcomes such that, with v voters, candidate k gets a plurality of the votes. Now, it is readily verified that the W_α partition Ω, and that the $W_\alpha{}^k$ partition Ω^k, i.e.,

$$\bigcup_{\alpha \in \Gamma} W_\alpha = \Omega, \text{ and } W_\alpha \cap W_\beta = \Phi \text{ (the empty set) for all } \alpha \ne \beta,$$
$$\text{with } \alpha, \beta \in \Gamma,$$
$$\bigcup_{\alpha \in \Gamma} W_\alpha{}^k = \Omega^k, \text{ and } W_\alpha{}^k \cap W_\beta{}^k = \Phi \text{ (the empty set) for all } \alpha \ne \beta,$$
$$\text{with } \alpha, \beta \in \Gamma.$$

We now restate Assumption 1:

a) $U(\bar{n}) = U(\bar{m})$ for all $\bar{n}, \bar{m} \in W_\alpha$ for each α; call this common value $U(\alpha)$;

b) $U^k(\bar{n}) = U^k(\bar{m})$ for all $\bar{n}, \bar{m} \in W_\alpha{}^k$ for each α, and k; call this common value $U^k(\alpha)$; and

c) $U(\alpha) = U^k(\alpha)$ for all α; call this common value U_α.

With this assumption expressions (1a) and (2a) become

$$E^\circ = \sum_{\alpha \in \Gamma} \sum_{\bar{n} \in W_\alpha} P(\bar{n})U(\alpha) = \sum_{\alpha \in \Gamma} P(W_\alpha)U_\alpha$$

and

$$E^k = \sum_{\alpha \in \Gamma} \sum_{\bar{n} \in W_\alpha{}^k} P^k(\bar{n})U^k(\alpha) = \sum_{\alpha \in \Gamma} P^k(W_\alpha{}^k)U_\alpha,$$

and so,

$$E^k - E^\circ = \sum_{\alpha \in \Gamma} [P^k(W_\alpha{}^k) - P(W_\alpha)]U_\alpha,$$

or, introducing the notation $q_\alpha{}^k = P^k(W_\alpha{}^k)$ and $q_\alpha{}^\circ = P(W_\alpha)$,

$$(3a) \qquad\qquad E^k - E^\circ = \sum_{\alpha \in \Gamma} (q_\alpha{}^k - q_\alpha{}^\circ)U_\alpha.$$

To prove Lemma 1 we restate Assumption 2:

If $\bar{n}^k = \bar{n} + \epsilon_k$, where $\epsilon_k = [0, 0, \cdots, 1, 0, \cdots, 0]$ with the 1 in the kth column, then $P^k(\bar{n}^k) = P(\bar{n})$; otherwise $P^k = 0$.

Proof of Lemma 1: Without loss of generality, let $k = 1$. First, we show that, if $\bar{n}^1 = \bar{n} + \epsilon_1$, then

$$\bar{n} \in W \Leftrightarrow \bar{n}^1 \in W_\alpha \cup W_{\alpha'}{}^1.$$

We proceed with the proof of this assertion as follows, recalling that from the statement of the lemma we assume that $1 \not\subset \alpha$:

$$\bar{n} \in W_\alpha \Leftrightarrow \bar{n} \in \Omega, \; n_j = n_k \text{ for } k, j \in \alpha, \text{ and } n_j > n_k \text{ for } j \in \alpha, k \not\subset \alpha;$$
$$\Leftrightarrow \bar{n} \in \Omega, \; n_j = n_k \text{ for } k, j \in \alpha, \text{ and } n_j > n_k \text{ for } j \in \alpha, 1 \neq$$
$$k \not\subset \alpha, n_j \geq n_1 + 1 \text{ for } j \in \alpha;$$
$$\Leftrightarrow \bar{n}^1 \in \Omega^1, \; n_j{}^1 = n_k{}^1 \text{ for } k, j \in \alpha, \text{ and } n_j{}^1 > n_k{}^1 \text{ for } j \in \alpha,$$
$$k \in \alpha', n_j{}^1 = n_1{}^1 \text{ for } j \in \alpha, \text{ or}$$
$$\bar{n}^1 \in \Omega^1, \; n_j{}^1 = n_k{}^1 \text{ for } k, j \in \alpha, \text{ and } n_j{}^1 > n_k{}^1 \text{ for } j \in \alpha,$$
$$1 \neq k \not\subset \alpha, n_j{}^1 > n_k{}^1 \text{ for } j \in \alpha;$$

$\Leftrightarrow \bar{n}^1 \in \Omega^1$, $n_j{}^1 = n_k{}^1$ for j, $k \in \alpha'$, $n_j{}^1 > n_k{}^1$ for $j \in \alpha'$, $k \not\subset \alpha'$, or

$\bar{n}^1 \in \Omega^1$, $n_j{}^1 = n_k{}^1$ for j, $k \in \alpha$, $n_j{}^1 > n_k{}^1$ for $j \in \alpha$, $k \not\subset \alpha$; and

$\Leftrightarrow \bar{n}^1 \in W_{\alpha'}{}^1$ or $\bar{n}^1 \in W_\alpha{}^1$.

Hence,

$$P(W_\alpha) = P^1(W_\alpha{}^1 \cup W_{\alpha'}{}^1)$$
$$= P^1(W_\alpha{}^1) + P^1(W_{\alpha'}{}^1),$$

since $W_\alpha{}^1$ and $W_{\alpha'}{}^1$ are disjoint; or

$$q_\alpha{}^\circ = q_\alpha{}^1 + q_{\alpha'}{}^1.$$

Proof of Lemma 2: First, from the definition of objective probabilities,

$$q_k{}^k = 1 - \sum_{\alpha \neq \{k\}} q_\alpha{}^k$$

and

$$q_k{}^\circ = 1 - \sum_{\alpha \neq \{k\}} q_\alpha{}^\circ,$$

and so,

$$q_k{}^k - q_k{}^\circ = \sum_{\alpha \neq \{k\}} (q_\alpha{}^\circ - q_\alpha{}^k) = \sum_{k \not\subset \alpha} (q_\alpha{}^\circ - q_\alpha{}^k) + \sum_{k \not\subset \alpha} (q_{\alpha'}{}^\circ - q_{\alpha'}{}^k)$$

$$= \sum_{k \not\subset \alpha} q_{\alpha'}{}^k + \sum_{k \not\subset \alpha} (q_{\alpha'}{}^\circ - q_{\alpha'}{}^k) \qquad \text{(from Lemma 1)}$$

$$= \sum_{k \not\subset \alpha} q_{\alpha'}. \qquad\qquad \text{Q.E.D.}$$

We proceed directly to the proof of Theorem 1 now by letting $\|\alpha\| =$ the number of elements in α, and,

$$U_\alpha = \frac{\sum_{i \in \alpha} U_i}{\|\alpha\|}, \qquad \overline{U}_\alpha = \frac{\sum_{i \in \alpha} (U_k - U_i)}{\|\alpha'\|},$$

where i is an integer.

Proof of Theorem 1: From expression (3a),

$$E^k - E^\circ = \sum_{\alpha \in \Gamma} (q^k - q_\alpha{}^\circ) U_\alpha$$

$$= \sum_{k \not\subseteq \alpha} (q_\alpha{}^k - q_\alpha{}^\circ) U_\alpha + \sum_{k \not\subseteq \alpha} (q_{\alpha'}{}^k - q_{\alpha'}{}^\circ) U_{\alpha'} + (q_k{}^k - q_k{}^\circ) U_k$$

$$= -\sum_{k \not\subseteq \alpha} q_{\alpha'}{}^k U_\alpha + \sum_{k \not\subseteq \alpha} (q_{\alpha'}{}^k - q_{\alpha'}{}^\circ) U_{\alpha'} + \sum_{k \in \alpha} q_{\alpha'}{}^\circ U_k$$

(from the two lemmas)

$$= \sum_{k \not\subseteq \alpha} q_{\alpha'}{}^k (U_{\alpha'} - U_\alpha) + \sum_{k \not\subseteq \alpha} q_{\alpha'}{}^\circ (U_k - U_{\alpha'}).$$

But,

$$U_{\alpha'} - U_\alpha = \frac{U_k + \sum_{i \in \alpha} U_i}{\|\alpha'\|} - \frac{\sum_{i \in \alpha} U_i}{\|\alpha\|}$$

$$= \frac{\|\alpha\| U_k + \|\alpha\| \sum_{i \in \alpha} U_i - (\|\alpha\| + 1) \sum_{i \in \alpha} U_i}{\|\alpha\| \quad \|\alpha'\|}$$

$$= \frac{\|\alpha\| U_k - \sum_{i \in \alpha} U_i}{\|\alpha\| \cdot \|\alpha'\|} = \frac{\sum_{i \in \alpha} (U_k - U_i)}{\|\alpha\| \cdot \|\alpha'\|} = \frac{\overline{U}_\alpha}{\|\alpha\|}.$$

And,

$$U_k - U_{\alpha'} = U_k - \frac{U_k + \sum_{i \in \alpha} U_i}{\|\alpha'\|} = \frac{\|\alpha\| U_k - \sum_{i \in \alpha} U_i}{\|\alpha'\|}$$

$$= \frac{\sum_{i \in \alpha} (U_k - U_i)}{\|\alpha'\|} = \overline{U}_\alpha.$$

Thus,

$$E^k - E^\circ = \sum_{k \not\subseteq \alpha} q_{\alpha'}{}^k \frac{\overline{U}_\alpha}{\|\alpha\|} + \sum_{k \not\subseteq \alpha} q_{\alpha'}{}^\circ \overline{U}_\alpha$$

$$= \sum_{k \not\subseteq \alpha} \left(q_{\alpha'}{}^\circ + \frac{q_{\alpha'}{}^k}{\|\alpha\|} \right) \overline{U}_\alpha. \qquad \text{Q.E.D.}$$

The proofs of Corollaries 1 and 2 are unnecessary since their validity follows directly from Theorem 1 and Assumptions 3 and 4.

Appendix II

Proof of expression (33) and Theorem 2 from Section 5

WHEN c, the number of candidates, equals 3, let,

$$\Omega_v = \{(n_1, n_2, n_3) \mid n_1 + n_2 + n_3 = v,\ n_i \geq 0 \text{ for } i = 1, 2, 3\}.$$

Thus, Ω_v is the set of all possible outcomes with v voters and three candidates. We let W_α^v be the set of outcomes with v voters in which α wins. As before, we let the notation $\|A\|$ denote the number of elements in the set A, so that $\|\alpha\|$ is the order of a tie, α, and $\|W_\alpha^v\|$ is the number of possible ways in which the set of candidates in α can tie for first place, assuming v voters.

Lemma: For $c = 3$, and $\|\alpha\| = 2$, $\|W_\alpha^{v+6}\| = \|W_\alpha^v\| + 1$.

Proof: With $c = 3$, there are three possible ties of order 2: $\{1, 2\}$, $\{1, 3\}$, and $\{2, 3\}$. No loss of generality is incurred if we assume that $\alpha = \{1, 2\}$, since an equivalent proof applies to the remaining two possibilities. Our proof is divided now into cases:

Case (i): $v = 0, 1,$ or 3.

If $v = 0, 1,$ or 3, then $W_\alpha^v = \Phi$, the empty set, so $\|W_\alpha^v\| = 0$. Now, if $v = 0$, then $v + 6 = 6$. But $W_{12}^6 = \{(3, 3, 0)\}$; so $\|W_\alpha^6\| = 1$. If $v = 1$, then $v + 6 = 7$. But $W_{12}^7 = \{(3, 3, 1)\}$; so $\|W_\alpha^6\| = 1$. Finally, if $v = 3$, then $v + 6 = 9$. But $W_{12}^9 = \{(4, 4, 1)\}$; so $\|W_\alpha^9\| = 1$. Hence, for $v = 0, 1,$ or 3, $\|W_\alpha^v\| = 0$ and $\|W_\alpha^{v+6}\| = 1$, assuming that $\|\alpha\| = 2$, so the lemma holds.

Case (ii): $v \neq 0, 1,$ or 3.

We can order the $\|W_\alpha^v\|$ members of W_α^v, and write them as

the ith member is $(k_i, k_i, v - 2k_i)$, where $\dfrac{v}{3} < k_i \leq \dfrac{v}{2}$ for each i, and $k_i = k_{i+1}$ for $1 \leq i \leq \|W_\alpha^v\| - 1$.

Now, we form the set Ψ, consisting of all vectors of the following form:

(a) $(k_i + 3, k_i + 3, v - 2k_i)$ for some $1 \le i \le \|W_\alpha{}^v\|$,

or

(b) $(k_i + 2, k_i + 2, v + 2 - 2k_i)$ for some $1 \le i \le \|W_\alpha{}^v\|$.

We claim that $W^{v+6} = \Psi$. Before proving this assertion, we show that Ψ has exactly $\|W_\alpha{}^v\| + 1$ distinct elements. Clearly, the $\|W_\alpha{}^v\|$ vectors of the form (b) are distinct from each other since each of the k_i are distinct. We show now that adding elements of the form (a) to those of the form (b) so as to generate the set Ψ adds only one new and distinct element. First, consider the element $(k_1 + 3, k_1 + 3, v - 2k_1)$. Since $k_1 \ge k_i$ for all i implies that $k_1 + 3 > k_i + 2$ for all i, $(k_1 + 3, k_1 + 3, v - 2k_1)$ is distinct from any element of the form (b) $(k_i \ge k_i$ for all i since, by definition, $k_i = k_{i+1} + 1)$. But if $i \ne 1$, then $k_i + 3 = (k_i + 1) + 2 = k_{i-1} + 2$. Hence $(k_i + 3, k_i + 3, v - 2k_i) = (k_{i-1} + 2, k_{i-1} + 2, v + 2 - 2k_{i-1})$, $i \ne 1$, so that this element is not an element distinct from those which can be written as (b). Thus, Ψ contains the $\|W_\alpha{}^v\|$ elements of the form (b) plus the element $(k_1 + 3, k_1 + 3, v - 2k_1)$, or $\|W_\alpha{}^v\| + 1$ elements.

We now prove that $W_\alpha{}^{v+6} = \Psi$ by showing first that $\Psi \subseteq W_\alpha{}^{v+6}$ and then that $W_\alpha{}^{v+6} \subseteq \Psi$. To show that $\Psi \subseteq W_\alpha{}^{v+6}$, consider an element of Ψ of the form (a). We can easily show that this element is in Ω_{v+6}; and, since $v/3 < k_i \le v/2$, $v/3 + 3 < k_i + 3 \le v/2 + 3 \Rightarrow (v + 9)/3 < k_i + 3 \le (v + 6)/2 \Rightarrow (v + 6)/3 < k_i + 3 \le (v + 6)/2$ (since $v + 6 < v + 9$). So this element satisfies our definition of $W_\alpha{}^{v+6}$ and is thereby in $W_\alpha{}^{v+6}$. Similarly, if we pick an element in Ψ of the form (b), say $(k_i + 2, k_i + 2, v + 2 - 2k_i)$, it is easily seen that this element is in Ω_{v+6}; and, since $v/3 < k_i \le v/2 \Rightarrow (v + 6)/3 < k_i + 2 \le (v + 4)/2 \le (v + 6)/2$, this element is in $W_\alpha{}^{v+6}$. This proves that $\Psi \subseteq W_\alpha{}^{v+6}$.

Now pick an arbitrary element of $W_\alpha{}^{v+6}$. This element must be of the form $(m, m, v + 6 - 2m)$ with $(v + 6)/3 < m \le (v + 6)/2$. Then, $v/3 + 2 < m \le v/2 + 3 \Rightarrow v/3 < m - 2 \le v/2 + 1$. Now, if $v/3 < m - 2 \le v/2$, then $(m, m, v + 6 - 2m) \in \Psi$, for it is of the form (b), where $k_i = m - 2$. So assume that this is not the case. Then $v/2 < m - 2 \le v/2 + 1 \Rightarrow$

(4a) $\dfrac{v}{2} - 1 < m - 3 \le \dfrac{v}{2}.$

Now if $v > 6$, then $3v - 2v > 6 \Rightarrow 3v - 6 > 2v \Rightarrow 3(v - 2) > 2v \Rightarrow (v - 2)/2 > v/3 \Rightarrow v/2 - 1 > v/3$, so in this case (4a) becomes

$$\frac{v}{3} < \frac{v}{2} - 1 < m - 3 \le \frac{v}{2},$$

and hence $(m, m, v + 6 - 2m) \in \Psi$, and is of the form (a), where $k_i = m - 3$. If $v \leq 6$, then, since $m - 3$ is an integer and $v/2 - 1$ may not be an integer, $v/2 - 1 < m - 3 \Rightarrow |[v/2 - 1]| + 1 \leq m - 3$, where $|[x]|$ denotes the greatest integer in x.

For $v \neq 0, 1$, or 3, and for $v \leq 6$ it is easily verified that

$$\frac{v}{3} < \left|\left[\frac{v}{2} - 1\right]\right| + 1.$$

Hence, for $v \leq 6$, we again get $v/3 < m - 3 \leq v/2$. So, for any $v \neq 0, 1$, or 3 $(m, m, v + 6 - 2m) \in \Psi$, and is of the form (a), where $k_i = m - 3$. Thus, we have shown that $W_\alpha^{v+6} \subseteq \Psi$.

Therefore, for case (ii), $W_\alpha^{v+6} = \Psi$. But since we have seen that Ψ has $\|W_\alpha^v\| + 1$ elements,

$$\|W_\alpha^{v+6}\| = \|W_\alpha^v\| + 1. \qquad \text{Q.E.D.}$$

We now state and prove one additional lemma.

Lemma: For $c = 3$, and $\|\alpha\| = 2$, let $\Gamma_v = \|W_\alpha^v\|$. Then,

$$\Gamma_v = \left|\left[\frac{v}{6}\right]\right| \text{ if } v \equiv 0, 1, \text{ or } 3 \pmod 6$$

and

$$\Gamma_v = \left|\left[\frac{v}{6}\right]\right| + 1 \text{ if } v \equiv 2, 4, \text{ or } 5 \pmod 6.$$

Proof (by induction): We write v as

$$v = 6n + k, \text{ where } 0 \leq k \leq 5.$$

Then,

$$\text{if } k = 0, 1, \text{ or } 3, v \equiv 0, 1, \text{ or } 3 \pmod 6$$

and

$$\text{if } k = 2, 4, \text{ or } 5, v \equiv 2, 4, \text{ or } 5 \pmod 6.$$

By inspection, we see that $W_\alpha^0 = W_\alpha^1 = W_\alpha^3 = \Phi$, the empty set, so $\Gamma_0 = \Gamma_1 = \Gamma_3 = 0$. $W_\alpha^2 = \{(1, 1, 0)\}$, $W_\alpha^4 = \{(2, 2, 0)\}$, $W_\alpha^5 = \{(2, 2, 1)\}$, so $\Gamma_2 = \Gamma_4 = \Gamma_5 = 1$. Hence, when $n = 0$ the result holds. Now assume that the result holds for $n = n_o$, i.e., when $v_o = 6n_o + k$, with $0 \leq k \leq 5$. Then, if $n = n_o + 1, v = 6(n_o + 1) + k$ or $v = (6n_o + k) + 6 = v_o + 6$. So from the previous lemma,

$$\Gamma_v = \Gamma_{v_o+6} = \Gamma_{v_o} + 1.$$

Since this result holds for $n = n_o$,

$$\Gamma_{v_o} = \left\| \left[\frac{v_o}{6} \right] \right\| = n_o \text{ if } k = 0, 1, \text{ or } 3$$

and

$$\Gamma_{v_o} = \left\| \left[\frac{v_o}{6} \right] \right\| + 1 = n_o + 1 \text{ if } k = 2, 4, \text{ or } 5.$$

Hence,

$$\Gamma_v = n_o + 1 = n = \left\| \left[\frac{v}{6} \right] \right\| \text{ if } k = 0, 1, \text{ or } 3$$

and

$$\Gamma_v = (n_o + 1) + 1 = n + 1 = \left\| \left[\frac{v}{6} \right] \right\| + 1 \text{ if } k = 2, 4, \text{ or } 5.$$

So the result holds for $n = n_o + 1$. By mathematical induction, the lemma is proved.   Q.E.D.

Now, suppose that we assume a uniform distribution over all outcomes so that the probability of a two-way tie between candidates 1 and 2 is the number of ways such a tie can occur, divided by the total number of possible outcomes. Since the total number of possible outcomes with $c = 3$ is $\|\Omega_v\| = (v + 1)(v + 2)/2$, then, if $\|\alpha\| = 2$, from the lemma, with $q_\alpha^0 = P(W_\alpha^v)$,

$$q_\alpha^0 = \begin{cases} \dfrac{2\left\| \left[\dfrac{v}{6} \right] \right\|}{(v + 1)(v + 2)} & \text{if } v \equiv 0, 1, \text{ or } 3 \pmod 6, \\[4mm] \dfrac{2\left(\left\| \left[\dfrac{v}{6} \right] \right\| + 1 \right)}{(v + 1)(v + 2)} & \text{if } v \equiv 2, 4, \text{ or } 5 \pmod 6, \end{cases}$$

or, writing $v = 6n + k$ with $0 \le k \le 5$, as before,

$$q_\alpha^0 = \begin{cases} \dfrac{2n}{(v + 1)(v + 2)} & \text{if } k = 0, 1, \text{ or } 3, \\[4mm] \dfrac{2(n + 1)}{(v + 1)(v + 2)} & \text{if } k = 2, 4, \text{ or } 5. \end{cases}$$

And, since $(v + 1) = 6n + (k + 1)$, if $1 \in \alpha$, we can show that

$$q_\alpha^1 = \begin{cases} \dfrac{2n}{(v+1)(v+2)} & \text{if } k+1 = 1, \text{ or } 3, \text{ i.e., if } k = 0, \text{ or } 2, \\[2mm] \dfrac{2(n+1)}{(v+1)(v+2)} & \text{if } k+1 = 2, 4, \text{ or } 5, \text{ i.e., if } k = 1, 3, \text{ or } 4, \\[2mm] \dfrac{2(n+1)}{(v+1)(v+2)} & \text{if } k+1 = 6, \text{ i.e., if } k = 5. \end{cases}$$

This result follows because, from Assumption 2, we know that there are still only $(v+1)(v+2)/2$ outcomes in Ω_v^1 with positive probabilities of occurrence. Using the assumption of equiprobability and applying the previous lemma, we obtain the above result.

It follows, then, that

$$q_\alpha^{\,0} + q_\alpha^{\,1} = \begin{cases} \dfrac{4n}{(v+1)(v+2)} & \text{if } k = 0, \\[2mm] \dfrac{2n + 2(n+1)}{(v+1)(v+2)} & \text{if } k = 1, 2, \text{ or } 3, \\[2mm] \dfrac{4(n+1)}{(v+1)(v+2)} & \text{if } k = 4, \text{ or } 5. \end{cases}$$

Now, let us write $v = 3n_1 + k_1$, where $-2 \leq k_1 \leq 0$. Then,

$$k = 0,\ k_1 = 0, \text{ and } 3n_1 = 6n \Rightarrow n = \frac{n_1}{2},$$

$$k = 1,\ k_1 = -2, \text{ and } 3n_1 - 2 = 6n + 1 \Rightarrow n = \frac{n_1 - 1}{2},$$

$$k = 2,\ k_1 = -1, \text{ and } 3n_1 - 1 = 6n + 2 \Rightarrow n = \frac{n_1 - 1}{2},$$

$$k = 3,\ k_1 = 0, \text{ and } 3n_1 = 6n + 3 \Rightarrow n = \frac{n_1 - 1}{2},$$

$$k = 4,\ k_1 = -2, \text{ and } 3n_1 - 2 = 6n + 4 \Rightarrow n = \frac{n_1 - 2}{2},$$

$$k = 5,\ k_1 = -1, \text{ and } 3n_1 - 1 = 6n + 5 \Rightarrow n = \frac{n_1 - 2}{2},$$

and we can see that

$$q_\alpha^{\,0} + q_\alpha^{\,1} = \frac{2n_1}{(v+1)(v+2)} \quad \text{for all } k_1.$$

But now $(v+2)/3 = (3n_1 + k_1 + 2)/3 = n_1 + (k_1 + 2)/3$. And since $-2 \leq k_1 \leq 0,\ 0 \leq (k_1 + 2)/3 \leq 1$; so

$$\left[\!\!\left[\frac{v+2}{3} \right]\!\!\right] = n_1,$$

and we can write

$$q_\alpha{}^\circ + q_\alpha{}^1 = \frac{2\left[\dfrac{v+2}{3}\right]}{(v+1)(v+2)}.$$

This result holds whether $\alpha = \{1, 2\}$ or $\{1, 3\}$; hence, from Corollary 2, if we let $\Pi_3 = E^1 - E^\circ$, then $\Pi_3 \cong (q_{12}{}^\circ + q_{12}{}^1)(U_1 - U_2)/2 + (q_{13}{}^\circ + q_{13}{}^1)(U_1 - U_3)/2 = (q_{12}{}^\circ + q_{12}{}^1)(2U_1 - U_2 - U_3)/2$. If $U_3 = (1 - \lambda)U_2 + \lambda U_1$, a convex combination of U_1 and U_2, then

$$\begin{aligned}
\Pi_3 &= \frac{(q_{12}{}^\circ + q_{12}{}^1)}{2}[2U_1 - \lambda U_1 - (1 - \lambda)U_2 - U_2] \\
&= (q_{12}{}^\circ + q_{12}{}^1)[(2 - \lambda)U_1 - (2 - \lambda)U_2]/2 \\
&= (q_{12}{}^\circ + q_{12}{}^1)[(2 - \lambda)(U_1 - U_2)]/2.
\end{aligned}$$

And, if $c = 2$, and we let the utilities for the two candidates be U_1 and U_2, then, if $\Pi_2 = E^1 - E^\circ$,

$$\Pi_2 = (q_{12}{}^\circ + q_{12}{}^1)(U_1 - U_2)/2.$$

Proof of Theorem 2: We have shown above, in the previous lemma, that for three candidates,

$$q_{12}{}^\circ + q_{12}{}^1 = \frac{2\left[\dfrac{v+2}{3}\right]}{(v+1)(v+2)}, \, c = 3.$$

In Section 5 we show that for two candidates,

$$q_{12}{}^\circ + q_{12}{}^1 = 1/(v+1), \, c = 2.$$

Thus, from above,

$$\Pi_3 = \frac{(2 - \lambda)\left[\dfrac{v+2}{3}\right]}{(v+1)(v+2)}(U_1 - U_2)$$

and

$$\Pi_2 = \frac{1}{2(v+1)}(U_1 - U_2),$$

and so,

$$\Pi_3 \geq \Pi_2 \Leftrightarrow \frac{\left[\dfrac{v+2}{3}\right](2 - \lambda)(U_1 - U_2)}{(v+1)(v+2)} \geq \frac{(U_1 - U_2)}{2(v+1)}$$

$$\Leftrightarrow \frac{\left[\left[\dfrac{v+2}{3}\right]\right](2-\lambda)}{(v+2)} \geq \frac{1}{2}$$

$$\Leftrightarrow 2\left[\left[\frac{v+2}{3}\right]\right](2-\lambda) \geq (v+2).$$

Writing $v = 3n + k$, with $-2 \leq k \leq 0$, we get

$$
\begin{aligned}
\Pi_3 \geq \Pi_2 &\Leftrightarrow 2n(2-\lambda) \geq 3n + k + 2 \\
&\Leftrightarrow 4n - 2n\lambda \geq 3n + k + 2 \\
&\Leftrightarrow 2n\lambda \leq n - k - 2 \\
&\Leftrightarrow \lambda \leq (n - k - 2)/2n.
\end{aligned}
$$

Observe now, from l' Hopital's rule, that

$$\lim_{n \to \infty} (n - k - 2)/2n = \tfrac{1}{2},$$

and as $n \to \infty$, $v \to \infty$; hence, as $v \to \infty$, $\Pi_3 \geq \Pi_2 \Leftrightarrow \lambda \leq \tfrac{1}{2}$. But $U_3 = (1 - \lambda)U_2 + \lambda U_1 + \lambda(U_1 - U_2)$. If $\lambda \leq \tfrac{1}{2}$, then $U_3 \leq U_2 + (U_1 - U_2)/2$, or, equivalently, $2U_3 \leq U_2 + U_1 - U_2 = U_2 + U_1$, or, equivalently,

$$(U_3 - U_2) \leq (U_1 - U_3),$$

which is the result we wanted to show. The second part of the theorem is simply the contrapositive of the first statement, hence the theorem is proved.

Appendix III

Proof of result in Section 6

FIRST, to prove our result, we consider only the probability $q_{12}{}^\circ$, noting that a parallel analysis of $q_{12}{}^1$, $q_{13}{}^1$, and $q_{13}{}^\circ$ can be conducted. Observe now that $q_{12}{}^\circ$ depends on the citizen's estimate of the probability that a certain outcome, a first-place tie between candidates 1 and 2, characterizes the election. Assume that the citizen behaves as if he estimates a probability density function which is defined on the space of outcomes Ω. To represent this function, consider the usual two-dimensional coordinate system with origin $(0, 0)$, and let the element Ω which represents a three-way tie be denoted $(0, 0)$. Let $g\,(x - \mu)$, $x = (x_1, x_2)$ be the subjectively estimated density function, and assume that $g(x - \mu)$ is symmetric, continuously differentiable, with mean $\mu = (\mu_1, \mu_2)$. By symmetry we mean that $g(x') = g(x'')$ for all x' and x'' such that $\|x' - \mu\| = \|x'' - \mu\|$, where $\|a - b\|$ denotes the distance between a and b. Thus, the constant probability contours of $g(x - \mu)$ are circles. The relationship of Ω, the coordinate space, and $g(x - \mu)$ is illustrated in Figure 2.5.

Now, we define the sets T and $\bar{T}$,

$$T = \{x \mid \| x - \mu \| \leq Z\}$$
$$\bar{T} = \{x \mid \| x - \mu \| > Z\}$$

where Z is some real positive number, and we assume that

$$\frac{\partial g(x - \mu)}{\partial x_i} \text{ exists for all } x \in T$$
$$= 0 \text{ for all } x \in \bar{T}$$

and

$$g(x - \mu) \geq 0 \text{ for all } x \in T$$
$$= 0 \text{ for all } x \in \bar{T}.$$

Thus, $g(x - \mu)$ is a bounded density function. This permits us to vary the mean of $g(x - \mu)$ in the spaces Ω and Ω^1 without varying its functional form where Z is sufficiently small.

Consider now the probability $q_{12}°$ and Figure 2.5. The line L_1 represents all first-place ties between candidates 1 and 2 and is assumed to be continuous for large v. The circle is the outer boundary of $g(x - \mu)$, and, therefore, has a radius of Z. Finally, S_2 and S_1 are the points of intersection between L_1 and the circle $\|x - \mu\| = Z$. Note that $S_2 \geq S_1$. Now

Figure 2.5. Relationship of Ω, the coordinate space, and $g(x - \mu)$

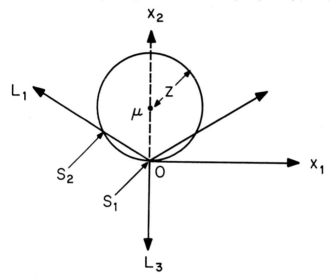

observe that $q_{12}°$ equals the area under $g(x - \mu)$ from S_1 to S_2. Let the distance along L_1 from 0 be denoted by t_1. Since the angle between L_1 and x_1 is 120°,

$$x_1 = \sqrt{3t_1}/2$$

and

$$x_2 = t_1/2.$$

Thus,

$$q_{12}° = \int_{S_1}^{S_2} g(\sqrt{3t_1}/2 - \mu_1, t_1/2 - \mu_2)dt._1$$

Since we consider only variations in μ along the x_2 axis, assume now that $\mu = (0, \mu_2)$, which is equivalent to assuming that candidate 1 gains support equally from citizens who previously considered voting for either candidate 2 or candidate 3. Hence,

$$q_{12}{}^\circ = \int_{S_1}^{S_2} g(\sqrt{3}t_1/2,\ t_1/2 - \mu_2)dt_1.$$

We now examine $\partial q_{12}{}^\circ/\partial\mu_2$ since this rate of change represents the change in $q_{12}{}^\circ$ as the citizen's subjective estimate of candidate 1's fortunes increases. First, let

$$g' = \frac{\partial g(x - \mu)}{\partial x_1}$$

and g_{S_1} and g_{S_2} be $g(\sqrt{3}t_1/2,\ t_1/2 - \mu_2)$ evaluated at S'_1 and S'_2 respectively. By standard mathematical procedures (see Liebnitz's Rule) we can show that

$$\partial q_{12}{}^\circ/\partial\mu_2 = -\int_{S_1}^{S_2} g' dt_1 + \frac{\partial S_2}{\partial\mu_2} g_{S_2'} - \frac{\partial S_1}{\partial\mu_2} g_{S_1}$$

since S_1 and S_2 are vector valued functions of the vector μ.

To evaluate $\partial q_{12}{}^\circ/\partial\mu_2$ we examine all admissable values of μ. First, let $\mu_2 < Z$. Obviously $\partial S_1/\partial\mu_2 = 0$ since $S_1 = 0$, a constant. Thus,

$$\partial q_{12}{}^\circ/\partial\mu_2 = -2\int_{0}^{S_2} g' dt_1 - 2\frac{\partial S_2}{\partial\mu_2} g_{S_2}.$$

Now consider the line $x_2 = \mu_2$, a horizontal line, parallel to the x_1-axis, passing through the point μ. Obviously, this line intersects L at some point, say Z_0. This point is illustrated in Figure 2.6. The distance from 0 to Z_0 is, by construction, $2\mu_2$, whereas the distance from μ to Z_0 is $\sqrt{3}\mu_2$. Thus, for $\mu_2 < Z/\sqrt{3}$, $Z_0 < S_2$, and for $\mu_2 = Z/\sqrt{3}$, $Z_0 = S_2$. Note that the point Z_0 occurs where a line perpendicular to the x_1-axis is a tangent of one of g's constant probability contours. This follows from the circular symmetry of g, and the fact that μ and Z_0 both lie on $x_2 = \mu_2$. Obviously, therefore,

$$g' > 0,\ \text{for}\ t_1 > Z,$$
$$g' = 0,\ \text{for}\ t_1 = Z,$$
$$g' < 0,\ \text{for}\ t_1 > Z.$$

We now show that for some μ_2 less than $Z/\sqrt{3}$ but greater than 0, $\partial q_{12}{}^\circ/\partial\mu_2 = 0$, which by inspection is taken to be a maximum for $q_{12}{}^\circ$. To do this we evaluate $\partial q_{12}{}^\circ/\partial\mu_2$ for $\mu_2 = 0$, and then for $\mu_2 = Z/\sqrt{3}$. If $\mu_2 = 0$, then $Z_0 = 0$; so, from the first inequality above,

$$\int_{0}^{S_2} g' dt_1 < 0,$$

Figure 2.6. Intersection of $x_2 = \mu_2$ and L

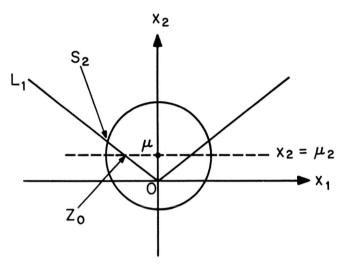

or, equivalently,

$$-\int_0^{S_2} g'\,dt_1 > 0, \text{ for } \mu_2 = 0.$$

Also, it is obvious that, for $\mu_2 = 0$, $\partial S_2/\partial \mu_2 > 0$, so that

$$\partial q_{12}{}^\circ/\partial \mu_2 > 0, \quad \text{when } \mu_2 = 0.$$

Observe, however, that as μ_2 approaches $Z/\sqrt{3}$, Z_0 approaches S_2, so that, for $\mu_2 = Z/\sqrt{3}$,

$$-\int_0^{S_2} g'\,dt_1 < 0,$$

and it is easily verified for the conditions specified that $\partial S_2/\partial \mu_2 = 0$; so

$$\partial q_{12}{}^\circ/\partial \mu_2 < 0, \quad \text{for } \mu_2 = Z/\sqrt{3}.$$

Thus, from the continuity of our functions,

$$\partial q_{12}{}^\circ/\partial \mu_2 = 0, \text{ for some } 0 < \mu_2 < Z/\sqrt{3}.$$

This demonstrates that some value of μ other than 0 maximizes $q_{12}{}^\circ$. For completeness, however, we examine $\mu_2 > Z/\sqrt{3}$. First, if $Z/\sqrt{3} < \mu_2 \leq Z$, it is readily verified that

$$-\int_0^{S_2} g' dt_1 < 0$$

and that $\partial S_2/\partial \mu_2 < 0$; so $\partial q°_{12}/\partial \mu_2 < 0$. Finally, if $\mu_2 > Z$,

$$-\int_{S_1}^{S_2} g' dt_1 < 0$$

since $Z_0 > S_2$. And it is obvious that

$$\partial S_1/\partial \mu_2 > 0, \text{ and } \partial S_2/\partial \mu_2 < 0,$$

and so again, $\partial q_{12}°/\partial \mu_2 < 0$ for all $\mu_2 > Z$, such that S_1 and S_2 exist. If S_1 and S_2 do not exist, $q_{12}° = 0$. Thus, the interval $(0, Z/\sqrt{3})$ is the unique interval along x_2 such that $\partial q_{12}°/\partial \mu_2 = 0$ and $q_{12}°$ is maximized. Similarly, this proves that $q_{12}{}^1$, $q_{13}°$, and $q_{13}{}^1$ are maximized for some $\mu_2 \neq 0$ so that $E^1 - E°$ is maximized for some $\mu_2 \neq 0$.

Models of Coalition Formation in Voting Bodies

3 Steven J. Brams,
New York University, and
William H. Riker,
University of Rochester

Introduction

DESPITE many recent attempts to look at political processes in dynamic terms, little progress has been made in developing models for studying political change. Systems theory has not proved particularly useful in the sequential analysis of political behavior, and even explicitly developmental approaches have provided little more than a set of verbal categories against which time-dependent processes are supposed to be traced. The paucity of statistical analyses employing longitudinal data is probably in part attributable to the absence of dynamic models of political processes.

In this paper we shall develop some simple mathematical models for studying the dynamics of coalition-formation processes in voting bodies. In part our effort might be viewed as a refinement and extension of work begun by William H. Riker in *The Theory of Political Coalitions*,[1] though

This is a revised and expanded version of a paper presented at the Annual Meeting of the American Association for the Advancement of Science, Boston, Dec. 26–31, 1969; and at the Annual Meeting of the American Political Science Association, Los Angeles, Sept. 8–12, 1970. We wish to thank Alan D. Miller and G. William Sensiba for their comments and suggestions and the National Science Foundation, under grant no. GS-2798 to Steven J. Brams and grant no. 5–28680 to William H. Riker, for financial support.

[1] (New Haven: Yale University Press, 1962). For a review of different coalition theories and an evaluation of their applicability to the prediction of party coalitions in the Japanese Diet, see Michael Leiserson, "Factions and Coalitions in One-Party Japan: An Interpretation Based on the Theory of Games," *American Political Science Review*, LXII (Sept., 1968), esp. 784–86; for a more recent appraisal with an application to the Italian Parliament, see Robert Axelrod, *Conflict of Interest: A Theory of Divergent Goals with Applications to Politics* (Chicago: Markham, 1970); and for a test of different theories, with largely negative results, using data from several European parliaments, see Eric C. Browne, "Testing Theories of Coalition Formation in the European Context" (unpubl. paper, University of Strathclyde, n.d.). Relevant to the study of electoral coalitions is the theory, with applications to France, pre-

the scope of our present study will be much more limited than Riker's general theory. We shall restrict our analysis to the study of coalition-formation processes involving as active opponents only two *protocoalitions* (associations with too few members to be decisive alone), which vie for the support of uncommitted members in a voting body in order that they may become winning coalitions (which are decisive, given some decision rule). A subset of all winning coalitions that shall be distinguished in the subsequent analysis consists of those that are *minimal winning*, i.e., coalitions where the subtraction of a single member reduces them to (nonwinning) protocoalitions.

In our simplified models, we shall be interested in studying only the formation of winning coalitions including one or the other of the two protocoalitions, but not both. We assume that the two protocoalitions are totally at odds with each other and seek victory only through securing the commitment of uncommitted members and not through the switching of members' commitments from one protocoalition to the other. We thus preclude members of the two protocoalitions from combining with each other to form a winning coalition.

While we attach no magic to the number two, our assumption of two opposed protocoalitions provides a useful starting point for analysis. Empirically, it seems compatible with many winner-take-all electoral systems, which tend to reduce conflicts to those involving only two opponents. At a theoretical level, the assumption in the characteristic function form of *n*-person game theory that a coalition will inspire the formation of a counter-coalition, whose members can get at least as much and possibly more by banding together, provides some justification for viewing even *n*-person games ($n > 2$) as reducible to two-person games.

Our purpose in making these simplifying assumptions is to focus attention on the conflict between the two protocoalitions both striving to enlist the support of uncommitted members. We are particularly interested in exploring the possible calculations that leaders of the protocoalitions

---

sented in Howard Rosenthal, "Voting and Coalition Models in Election Simulations," in William D. Coplin (ed.), *Simulation in the Study of Politics* (Chicago: Markham, 1968), pp. 237–85; and Howard Rosenthal, "Political Coalition: Elements of a Model and the Study of French Legislative Elections," *Editions du Centre National de la Recherche Scientifique* (Paris, 1968), pp. 269–282. For an analysis of the 1964 presidential campaign from a coalition-theory perspective, see John H. Kessel, *The Goldwater Coalition: Republican Strategies in 1964* (Indianapolis: Bobbs-Merrill, 1968). Much diverse material on coalition behavior can be found in Sven Groennings, E. W. Kelly, and Michael Leiserson (eds.), *The Study of Coalition Behavior: Theoretical Perspectives and Cases from Four Continents* (New York: Holt, Rinehart, & Winston, 1970). While virtually all previous work takes existent winning coalitions as a point of departure, the analysis of this paper focuses on the dynamic aspects of bargaining *prior* to the victory of one coalition.

may make in trying to determine how much to offer the uncommitted members to join, and, conversely, the possible calculations the uncommitted members may make in trying to decide what a commitment is objectively worth.[2] For this purpose, we shall define several different concepts of payoff, reckoned in both pivots and probabilities and based on different assumptions about what values members seek to maximize and what combinatorial possibilities they consider to be those available from which to choose. From different calculations of the costs and benefits involved in uncommitted members' joining or not joining different protocoalitions, we shall draw inferences about the dynamic consequences following from the different assumptions of the different models by trying to ferret out patterns and regularities emerging from the calculations.

To illustrate the analysis, we shall trace these different concepts and assumptions through the operation of a ten-member body, with the decision rule being majority rule (six out of ten). Starting with no members in each of the two protocoalitions, we shall add one member to each protocoalition until one protocoalition reaches minimal winning size with six members and thereby becomes decisive, or both protocoalitions obtain commitments from five members and form two blocking coalitions that, with no uncommitted members remaining, deadlock decisions on the part of each other. It will be convenient to represent this coalition-formation process in a latticelike structure, and alternatively graphically, in order to draw out some implications of the concepts and assumptions that will help us to understand under what circumstances certain coalitions form rather than others.

We shall conclude with an illustrative application of some of the models to voting data in multiballot national party conventions. In particular, we shall try to show how the models can help us better to understand and to predict the occurrence of the "take-off" point in a convention when the so-called "bandwagon effect" sweeps the front-running candidate on to victory.

[2] For a most fruitful exploration of this question using the methods of economic analysis, see James S. Coleman, "The Marginal Utility of a Vote Commitment," *Public Choice*, V (Fall, 1968), 39–53. Coleman specifically dismisses game theory as a not-very-useful model for the study of collective decisions and instead uses probability theory as the basis for his formal analysis of voting decisions. The probabilistic models we shall develop later are closely related to those of Coleman, but we have also utilized game theory in terms of a modified version of the Shapley-Shubik index. A recent article by Coleman also bears on this analysis. See his "The Benefits of Coalition," *Public Choice*, VIII (Spring, 1970), 45–61, in which a probabilistic model is used to explore gains and losses associated with joining or not joining a coalition when vote trading is and is not allowed.

Calculating the Proportion of Pivots of Actors in a Voting Body

Background. Political analysts have been interested for some time in measuring the distribution of power among members of a collectivity (which may comprise one or more subcollectivities, such as voting bodies or individual actors, interrelated by specified decision rules) through the analysis of its decision rules. One of the first major approaches to this problem was made by L. S. Shapley in his development of a measure of the value of a game.[3] This measure was subsequently adapted by Shapley and Martin Shubik to measure the distribution of power in a collectivity from the number of positions each actor occupies in all permutations that give him the pivotal vote.[4] Shapley and Shubik used their index to measure the distribution of power among the President, members of the House of Representatives, and members of the Senate;[5] it has since been applied to the analysis of several voting bodies, including the United States Electoral College,[6] the House of Representatives,[7] the Supreme Court,[8] the French National Assembly,[9] the United Nations Security Council and General Assembly,[10] and the New York City Board of Estimate.[11]

Recently the index has come under the scrutiny of several analysts who have attacked its assumption of giving equal weight to all different orders

[3] "A Value for *n*-Person Games," in H. W. Kuhn and A. W. Tucker (eds.), *Contributions to the Theory of Games, II* Annals of Mathematical Studies, no. 28 (Princeton, N.J.: Princeton University Press, 1953), 307–17.

[4] "A Method for Evaluating the Distribution of Power in a Committee System," *American Political Science Review*, XLVIII (Sept., 1954), 787–92.

[5] *Ibid.*

[6] Irwin Mann and L. S. Shapley, "The A Priori Voting Strength of the Electoral College," in Martin Shubik (ed.), *Game Theory and Related Approaches to Social Behavior* (New York: John Wiley, 1964), pp. 151–64. See also Paul T. David, Ralph M. Goldman, and Richard C. Bain, *The Politics of National Party Conventions* (Washington, D.C.: Brookings Institution, 1960), p. 175, for the results of Mann and Shapley's calculations.

[7] William H. Riker and Donald Niemi, "The Stability of Coalitions on Roll Calls in the House of Representatives," *American Political Science Review*, LVI (March, 1962), 58–65.

[8] Glendon A. Schubert, *Quantitative Analysis of Judicial Behavior* (Glencoe, Ill.: Free Press, 1959), chap. 4.

[9] William H. Riker, "A Test of the Adequacy of the Power Index," *Behavioral Science*, VI (1959), 120–31.

[10] Gerhard Schwodiauer, "Calculation of A Priori Power Distributions for the United Nations," Research Memorandum No. 24 (Vienna: Institute for Advanced Studies, July, 1968).

[11] Samuel Krislov, "The Power Index, Reapportionment, and the Principle of One Man, One Vote," *Modern Uses of Logic in Law* (now *Jurimetrics Journal*), June 1965, pp. 37–44.

(permutations) of actors in the counting of pivots. Since the order in which actors join a coalition is often of slight significance, these critics argue that, instead of using permutations that enumerate all possible arrangements of members where order counts, a more reasonable measure of pivotalness can be constructed from counting a member's pivots in those combinations where his absence would make the coalition a losing one.[12]

We shall illustrate these different calculations and point out some consequences of using combinations versus permutations for the ten-member body. Our major concern, however, is not whether combinations or permutations more accurately mirror power realities in the calculation of pivots but lies instead in placing restrictions on coalitions that can form in a body. In actual voting bodies, certain protocoalitions of members never or only rarely agree (e.g., parties on the extreme left and extreme right), so it makes little sense to consider different combinations or permutations that include these protocoalitions on the same winning side of the pivot in the calculation of the number of pivots of the different actors.[13] Transferring this reasoning to our idealized conflict between two protocoalitions (e.g., political parties), each seeking the support of uncommitted members, we shall disallow the pivots each protocoalition might pick up by allying itself with the other: the power of each instead resides in its being able to pivot only with the support of uncommitted members; correspondingly, each uncommitted member may pivot only with the support of either protocoalition.

To be sure, a host of situational factors—including "uncommitted" members predisposed to one or the other of the two protocoalitions, crosscutting affiliations of members of the two protocoalitions that encourage switching from one to the other, third protocoalitions, and so on —will upset any strict correspondence this model might have to coalition formation in real voting bodies. Nevertheless, we feel it serves well enough as an approximation of the manner in which coalitions form in some actual bodies to render the calculations we shall describe useful in analyzing the dynamics of coalition formation. We shall try to support

[12] John F. Banzhaf III, "Weighted Voting Doesn't Work: A Mathematical Analysis," *Rutgers Law Review*, XIX (1965), 317–43; James S. Coleman, "Control of Collectivities and the Power of a Collectivity to Act," P-3902 (Santa Monica, Calif.: RAND Corporation, August, 1968); and Douglas W. Rae, "A Measure for the Decisiveness of Election Outcomes" (unpubl. paper, Yale University, 1968).
[13] The possibility of "irreconcilable" protocoalitions was recognized by Glendon Schubert in one of his calculations for a nine-member voting body. See his "The Power of Organized Minorities in a Small Group," *Administrative Science Quarterly*, IX (Sept., 1964), 142–43. See also Samuel Krislov, "Power and Coalition in a Nine-Man Body," *American Behavioral Scientist*, VI (April, 1963), 24–26.

this contention at the end of the paper in our analysis of voting data from national party conventions.

Lattice Calculations. In Figure 3.1 we have given the lattice of payoffs based on the proportion of pivots held by each protocoalition and uncommitted member when all *combinations* of members in minimal winning coalitions are considered equally likely (which in the absence of other information is an assumption useful as a first approximation). Before ex-

Figure 3.1. Lattice of pivot and incremental proportions using combinations

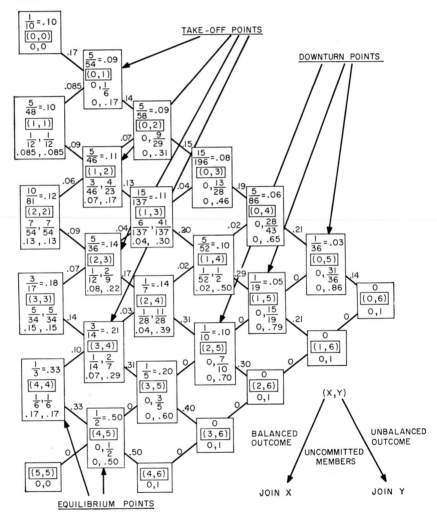

plaining the calculation of payoffs, we note that in each cell of the lattice the weights of each of the opposing protocoalitions are given by the ordered pair (X, Y), where X is equal to the number of members in the first protocoalition and Y is equal to the number of members in the second protocoalition.

As one moves diagonally downward and to the right in the lattice, uncommitted members singly join the second protocoalition (Y) in each lattice cell and move the process toward an unbalanced outcome (i.e., toward increasing disparity in the size of the two protocoalitions); as one moves diagonally downward and to the left in the lattice, uncommitted members join the first protocoalition (X) and move the process toward a balanced outcome. On the extreme left-hand side of the lattice, the two protocoalitions are always tied, as shown. Possible cells farther to the left giving outcomes in which X is the larger protocoalition are omitted since they are simply a mirror reflection of those already given in Figure 3.1.

Below the protocoalitions (X, Y) in each cell are given the fractional and decimal equivalent proportions of pivots that each protocoalition has. In calculating these proportions, we assume that each protocoalition or uncommitted member is pivotal only in those winning coalitions, including either X or Y but not both, where its subtraction from that coalition would reduce the coalition to one which is blocking or losing. For cell $(1, 2)$, for example, the single-member protocoalition (X) would on the average be pivotal 7 per cent of the time, and the two-member protocoalition (Y) would be pivotal 17 per cent of the time.

Each uncommitted member's proportion is given above each cell; the seven uncommitted members in the present example each have 11 per cent of the pivots. This percentage for an uncommitted member is greater than the percentage for the committed single-member protocoalition (X) because the uncommitted member is allowed to be pivotal in a coalition with X or Y and other uncommitted members, while X is not permitted to ally with Y in a winning coalition. The ideologically prepossessed X thus has fewer opportunities to act as a decisive force than has a "free-wheeling" uncommitted member who also has only one vote.

The 4 per cent difference between the 11 per cent proportion of pivots of an uncommitted member and the 7 per cent proportion of the one-member protocoalition (X) might be taken as a measure of the *cost of commitment* for X, corresponding to the opportunities he foregoes in disallowing himself pivots with the larger protocoalition, Y. As we shall see later, however, an uncommitted member's cost of joining at an early stage in the formation of protocoalitions may become a gain at a later stage. The opposing protocoalitions X and Y, on the other hand, suffer a loss in pivots at all stages by being prevented by the assumptions of the model from allying with each other. This loss we might call the *cost of*

Figure 3.2.   Lattice of pivot and incremental proportions using permutations

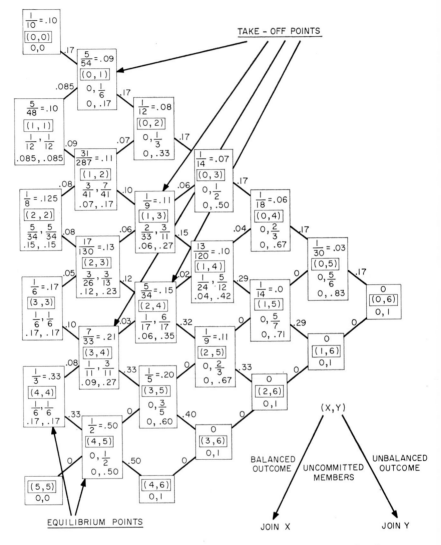

conflict (between X and Y), which tends to increase with the simultaneous increase in size of both protocoalitions. This cost is, of course, a gain to the uncommitted members whose pivotal role tends to be enhanced by the restriction on the two protocoalitions' combining with each other.

The lattice in Figure 3.2 gives pivot proportions when *permutations* of the protocoalitions and uncommitted members are considered equally likely. To show more precisely how the pivot proportions are calculated for both combinations and permutations, consider first the number of possible pivotal combinations for the single-member protocoalition of cell (1, 2), i.e., X (which, since it is the same weight as the uncommitted members, we shall distinguish as $1'$). Clearly, X of cell (1, 2) will be pivotal when five uncommitted members precede him and vote in his favor, as follows:

$$1 \quad 1 \quad 1 \quad 1 \quad 1 \quad [1'] \quad 1 \quad 1 \quad 2.$$

Since there are seven uncommitted members, there are $_7C_5 = 21$ *combinations* in which X can be pivotal.[14] Since there are $5! = 120$ ways of arranging the five uncommitted members who precede him in each combination, and $3! = 6$ ways of arranging the two uncommitted members and Y that follow him, there are a total of $_7C_5 \, 5!3! = 15,120$ *permutations* in which X can be pivotal. The term *pivotal*, however, does not mean that X necessarily casts the sixth (and decisive) vote for his side.[15]

For the two-member protocoalition (Y) of cell (1, 2), the possible permutations are as follows:

$$1 \quad 1 \quad 1 \quad 1 \quad [2] \quad 1 \quad 1 \quad 1 \quad 1' \qquad \binom{7}{4} \quad 4!4!$$

$$1 \quad 1 \quad 1 \quad 1 \quad 1 \quad [2] \quad 1 \quad 1 \quad 1' \qquad \binom{7}{5} \quad 5!3!.$$

For each uncommitted member we have

$$1' \quad 1 \quad 1 \quad 1 \quad 1 \quad [1] \quad 1 \quad 1 \quad 2 \qquad \binom{6}{4} \quad 5!3!$$

$$2 \quad 1 \quad 1 \quad 1 \quad [1] \quad 1 \quad 1 \quad 1 \quad 1' \qquad \binom{6}{3} \quad 4!4!.$$

[14] $_7C_5$ denotes the number of combinations that can be formed from 7 objects taken 5 at a time, or $7!/5!2! = 7\cdot6/2 = 21$. The exclamation point (!) indicates a factorial and means that the number it follows is to be multiplied by every positive integer smaller than itself (e.g., $3! = 3\cdot2\cdot1 = 6$). Below we write $_7C_5$ as $\binom{7}{5}$.

[15] By *pivotal* we mean that X is joined by a number of uncommitted members (five in this case) such that his subtraction would render the coalition losing. Unlike the text example, however, where we have shown five uncommitted members preceding the *pivot*, X, to illustrate the calculation of all possible arrangements, we do not need to assume that these uncommitted members precede X in their pledges of commitment or in the order of their voting, but rather that X is joined at some point in the process by five uncommitted members. Since a protocoalition's or uncommitted member's *pivotalness* depends only on the proportion of all combinations or permutations when his subtraction would reduce the winning coalition to a (losing) protocoalition, several actors may be *pivotal* in a winning coalition (i.e., the subtraction of any one of them would render the coalition losing). *Pivot*, then, is used only as a convenient descriptive term to indicate that an actor's presence is necessary to a coalition's remaining winning and not that the actor necessarily casts the final decisive vote.

In the above cases, the sum of the permutations for X ($_7C_5$ 5!3!), for Y ($_7C_4$ 4!4! + $_7C_5$ 5!3!), and for each uncommitted member ($_6C_4$ 5!3! + $_6C_3$ 4!4!), is the denominator for the pivot proportions. The numerators are the number of pivots for X, Y, and the uncommitted members individually. Thus for X the pivot proportion based on permutations is

$$\frac{\left[\binom{7}{5} 5!3!\right]}{\left[\binom{7}{5} 5!3!\right] + \left[\binom{7}{4} 4!4! + \binom{7}{5} 5!3!\right] + 7\left[\binom{6}{4} 5!3! + \binom{6}{3} 4!4!\right]}.$$

The pivot proportions based only on combinations are obtained in the same way when the figures for the combinations given above are not multiplied by the possible ways in which the members in each distinct combination can be ordered on both sides of the pivot. Thus, the proportion for X using combinations is

$$\frac{\left[\binom{7}{5}\right]}{\left[\binom{7}{5}\right] + \left[\binom{7}{4} + \binom{7}{5}\right] + 7\left[\binom{6}{4} + \binom{6}{3}\right]}.$$

For the lattice cells along the upper-right diagonal where X has zero members, of course, its subtraction from a winning coalition cannot render it losing so it is therefore never pivotal.

The decimal figures given along the lines connecting the lattice cells in Figures 3.1 and 3.2 indicate the incremental proportion of pivots that an uncommitted member adds by joining either the larger protocoalition, Y (moving the process diagonally downward and to the right), or the smaller protocoalition, X (moving the process diagonally downward and to the left). If the currency of voting power is reckoned in pivots, then this incremental proportion might well be used as an indicator of the *added value* in power that the new member can bring to the protocoalition — and what the protocoalition should be willing to expend in its resources, or commit in its expected payoffs, to entice the new member to join.

Thus, for lattice cell (1, 2) in Figure 3.1, the commitment of an uncommitted member to the smaller protocoalition (X) raises its pivot proportion from 0.07 at cell (1, 2) to 0.13 at cell (2, 2), or by an increment of 0.06; going from cell (1, 2) to cell (1, 3), on the other hand, an uncommitted member who joins Y increases Y's pivot proportion by 0.13.[16] The

[16] Taking into account not only these incremental gains but also the incremental losses incurred by the protocoalition that the uncommitted member does *not* join when the process moves to the next stage, allows us to define a concept of "net gain," whose implications have been developed in Steven J. Brams, "A Cost/Benefit Analy-

uncommitted member's pivot contribution is therefore greater if he joins
Y rather than X, which is the case for all lattice cells in Figures 3.1 and
3.2. If an uncommitted member's share in the benefits that accrue to the
protocoalition, should it win, is proportional to the proportion of pivots
that he contributes, then he can maximize this share by always following
a strategy of casting his lot with the larger protocoalition.[17]

Take-off Points. Yet it might not always be in the best interest of the uncommitted member to commit himself, even to the larger protocoalition,
Y. An uncommitted member at lattice cell (1, 2) in Figure 3.2, for example, is pivotal on the average 11 per cent of the time. By joining Y and
moving the process to cell (1, 3), he adds 0.10 proportion of pivots to Y's
pivot proportion, which is less than the proportion he has by remaining
uncommitted. At cell (1, 3), however, where an uncommitted member's
pivot proportion is also 0.11, it would pay for him to join Y, to which he
could add 0.15 proportion of pivots in moving the process to cell (1, 4).

Along the diagonals of the lattices in Figures 3.1 and 3.2 from the upper
left to the lower right, where the size of the smaller protocoalitions remains constant, we have indicated *take-off points* where the proportion of
pivots that an uncommitted member contributes to Y is for the first time
greater than the proportion he would have by remaining uncommitted.
At these points, in other words, it is rational for the uncommitted member to join Y. Prior to reaching these points, however, it is rational to hold
out. Only along the (4, 4)–(4, 6) diagonals in Figures 3.1 and 3.2 are there
no take-off points; instead, cells (4, 4) and (4, 5) are *equilibrium points*,
where the proportion of pivots received by an uncommitted member is
identical to the proportion he would receive by joining Y, suggesting
that an uncommitted member would be indifferent between remaining
uncommitted and committing himself to Y at these points.

The take-off points are those in the graphs of Figures 3.3a and 3.3b

---

sis of Coalition Formation in Voting Bodies," in Richard G. Niemi and Herbert F.
Weisberg (eds.), *Probability Models of Collective Decision-Making* (Columbus, Ohio:
Charles E. Merrill, forthcoming 1972).

[17] In a Markovian analysis of opinion change, Germain Kreweras postulated that
the probability of an uncommitted member's joining a protocoalition is a direct
function of the protocoalition's size and not the proportion of pivots that the uncommitted member contributes, which may be quite different. See his "A Model for
Opinion Change during Repeated Balloting," in Paul F. Lazarsfeld and Neil W.
Henry (eds.), *Readings in Mathematical Social Science* (Cambridge, Mass.: MIT
Press, 1968), pp. 174–91. For a discussion of the relationship between the size of a
protocoalition and its proportion of pivots, see William H. Riker and Lloyd S.
Shapley, "Weighted Voting: A Mathematical Analysis for Instrumental Judgments,"
in J. Roland Pennock and John W. Chapman (eds.), *Representation: Nomos X* (New
York: Atherton Press, 1968), pp. 199–216.

that lie just to the right of the indifference lines as one traces the buildup of Y while X is held constant. In these graphs we have connected the cells in Figures 3.1 and 3.2 where the smaller protocoalition (X) remains constant to illustrate the comparison between the usually rapidly rising offer that the larger protocoalition (Y) can make the uncommitted member — based on the proportion of pivots that the uncommitted member would contribute to Y — and the usually slowly rising (and eventually declining) amount that the uncommitted member can obtain from remaining uncommitted. Only as the process moves from lattice cell $(4, 4)$ to cell $(4, 5)$ along the lines of indifference in Figures 3.3a and 3.3b is the uncommitted member not penalized for holding out to the end, for at both points he is indispensable to Y's winning at cell $(4, 6)$ (or X's winning at cell $(6, 4)$, which is not shown on the lattice), or blocking at cell $(5, 5)$. These models support the commonsense proposition that it is rational for a member to hold out to the end only when almost all other members have previously committed themselves and he holds the

Figure 3.3. Pivot proportions for an uncommitted member in a ten-member body with majority rule

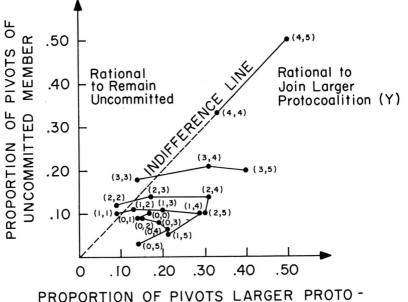

PROPORTION OF PIVOTS LARGER PROTO-
COALITION (Y) CAN OFFER UNCOMMITTED MEMBER

a. USING COMBINATIONS

Figure 3.3 (continued)

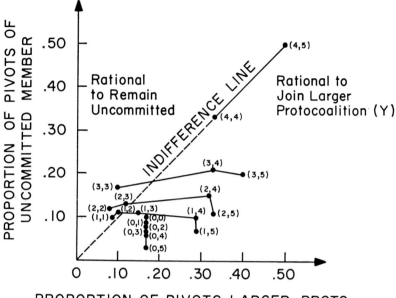

PROPORTION OF PIVOTS LARGER PROTO -
COALITION (Y) CAN OFFER UNCOMMITTED MEMBER

b. USING PERMUTATIONS

balance of power; otherwise, the larger protocoalition (Y) is favored in the world of perfect information we assume in our analysis.

What common sense does not provide, however, is advice, when one protocoalition has a substantial edge over the other, of exactly when it becomes rational to cast one's lot with the larger protocoalition, from which predictions and explanations based on the assumptions of our models can be offered.[18] Although the take-off points on the lattices and graphs differ somewhat as to the moment commitment is to be preferred over remaining uncommitted — depending on whether one uses combinations or permutations — in no case do the take-off points for the two sets of calculations vary by more than one cell along each of the diagonals of the lattices from upper left to lower right. More precisely, the take-off

---

[18] This is why delegates in national party conventions "may have to search frantically for clues as to the best time to make the jump [onto a bandwagon] and gain the greatest bargaining advantages for themselves." Nelson W. Polsby and Aaron Wildavsky, "Uncertainty and Decision-Making at the National Conventions," in Nelson W. Polsby, Robert A. Dentler, and Paul A. Smith (eds.), *Politics and Social Life: An Introduction to Political Behavior* (Boston: Houghton Miffin, 1963), p. 380.

points for combinations (Figure 3.1) occur one step earlier than for permutations (Figure 3.2), except along the (0, 0)–(0, 6) and (3, 3)–(3, 6) diagonals, which have the same take-off point (cells (0, 0) and (3, 4), respectively) for both combinations and permutations.

Thus, no matter whether or not one assumes combinations or permutations of actors are equiprobable, predictions as to when the larger protocoalition (Y) is likely to take off appear not to differ significantly (at least for our illustrative ten-member body). We caution, however, that other plausible assumptions can be made about the calculations that the uncommitted member might make. For example, instead of basing his commitment decision on the proportion of pivots *that he contributes* to Y — under the assumption that this will be his share of the benefits that accrue to Y — he may reason that his share of the pivots will be equal to the *same proportion* as that of all other members in the protocoalition that he joins.

For example, for lattice cell (2, 3) in Figure 3.1, the larger protocoalition of three members that he considers joining would have four members with his commitment; these four members at cell (2, 4) would have 0.39 proportion of the pivots, which averages out to about 0.10 proportion per member when divided equally among the four. Now an uncommitted member at cell (2, 3) can command 0.14 proportion of all pivots, so it would not pay for him to commit himself by this calculation, even though cell (2, 3) was a take-off point by our previous calculation based on the incremental proportion (not equal for all members of the protocoalition) of pivots that an uncommitted member contributes when he joins. Generally speaking, the calculation based on each protocoalition member's receiving an equal share of the pivots produces take-off points at a somewhat later stage along each diagonal (at lattice cell (2, 5) in the above case).

In developing theoretical models at this time, it seems less important to speculate on what might be the "right" set of assumptions in making the pivotal calculations and more important to be aware of the manner in which different assumptions may produce different results. We ought to be cognizant, that is, of the *consequences* of different assumptions.[19] In the above illustration, for example, dividing up the pivots of a protocoalition equally among all of its members in calculating the value of the protocoalition to an uncommitted member generally delays the point at which take-off occurs because this equal-share value will generally be less

---

[19] For a comparison of consequences flowing from different assumptions made in the coalition theory literature, see Steven J. Brams, "Positive Coalition Theory: The Relationship between Postulated Goals and Derived Behavior," in Cornelius P. Cotter *et al.* (eds.), *Political Science Annual: Conflict, Competition, and Coalitions*, IV (Indianapolis: Bobbs Merrill, forthcoming 1972).

than the incremental pivot contribution made by the uncommitted member who joins.

Downturn Points. So far most of our discussion has focused on the concept of take-off with little attention being directed toward the kinds of calculations made after the point of take-off is reached. Does the process snowball to an inexorable conclusion that always results in a lopsided victory for the larger protocoalition and therefore an unbalanced outcome? In political life obviously not, but how is it possible to achieve a balanced outcome, given the dynamic of our models?

Three explanations are suggested by the models. First, at the start most members might already be committed (e.g., at the equivalent of lattice cell (4, 4)), and a more or less balanced outcome is therefore assured. Second, the set of assumptions discussed previously that tends to delay take-off might be operative, so that when take-off does occur it cannot result in a large imbalance. The third possible explanation is more subtle and relates to the diminution in the incremental pivot contribution of uncommitted members who join the larger protocoalition *after* take-off, which tends to occur when the disparity in the size of the two protocoalitions is large. This occurs, for example, in the drop of an uncommitted member's incremental contribution from 0.29 to 0.21 as the process moves from cell (1, 4) to cells (1, 5) and (1, 6) for combinations in Figure 3.1. (For permutations in Figure 3.2, an uncommitted member's incremental contribution remains constant at 0.29 over this sequence, which is significant because it halts the previous escalating contributions of uncommitted members to the larger protocoalition along the (1, 1)–(1, 6) diagonal.) A drop in an uncommitted member's incremental contribution, though only slight, also characterizes the (0, 4)–(0, 5)–(0, 6) and the (2, 4)–(2, 5)–(2, 6) sequences in Figure 3.1.

What interpretation can be attached to this decline in the incremental contribution of an uncommitted member once the larger protocoalition has already attained a lead that has pushed it past the take-off point? This decline suggests that it may not always be rational for a coalition leader to bid progressively higher for each new member, because beyond a certain point when his protocoalition already enjoys a healthy lead the proportionate pivot contribution of the late-coming uncommitted member will not be as great as the contributions of one or more of the uncommitted members who joined before him.[20]

This notion seems reasonable when one considers that the late-coming uncommitted member who decides to join the larger protocoalition faces

[20] For a similar conclusion, see Coleman, "The Marginal Utility of a Vote Commitment," *op. cit.*, pp. 46–47, 54–55.

the risk, as the protocoalition approaches minimal winning size, of other
uncommitted members' joining before him and depriving him of the
opportunity of playing a decisive role in the victory. However, the declining benefits that the protocoalition leader might offer him at the final
stage—commensurate with his diminished incremental contribution to
the protocoalition's proportion of pivots—might not seem so reasonable
to the uncommitted member who has held out to the end only to see that
the other uncommitted members might beat him to the pivotal position.

After a presumed take-off point but before final victory for the leading
protocoalition, therefore, there may be some hesitation on the part of uncommitted members to accept the scaled-down benefits that it is rational
for the leader of the larger protocoalition to offer them. Victory may not
so ineluctably follow, with an unbalanced outcome the consequence,
when an uncommitted member must make downward revisions in his
expectations. In the extreme, the dismay produced by these downward
revisions may create an "underdog effect"—wherein uncommitted members are more likely to vote for a candidate when they expect him to lose
—as a countervailing force to the "bandwagon effect," wherein the uncommitted opt for the expected winner.[21] (We concede, however, that
this dismay may turn into anxiety at even further loss and work in the
opposite direction, producing a rush on the part of the uncommitted to
be the *next* to join, i.e., the bandwagon effect.) [22]

The point along any diagonal from the upper left to the lower right at
which the previously increasing pivot contributions of an uncommitted
member to the larger protocoalition (Y) begin to decline we shall hence-
forth call the *downturn point*. In Figure 3.1, the downturn points are cells
$(0, 5)$, $(1, 5)$, and $(2, 5)$, since an uncommitted member makes smaller incremental pivot contributions to Y following these points than before
them.[23] While at a take-off point it is to an individual's advantage to join
the larger protocoalition rather than hold out, an individual receives his
greatest payoff for a commitment made just prior to the downturn point
along any diagonal.[24]

---

[21] For an interesting analysis of the effect of these forces on the prediction of election
outcomes, see Herbert A. Simon, "Bandwagon and Underdog Effects of Election
Predictions," in his *Models of Man: Social and Rational* (New York: John Wiley,
1957), pp. 79–87.

[22] For a similar analysis of these contradictory forces, see Norman Frohlich, Joe A.
Oppenheimer and Oran R. Young, *Political Leadership and Collective Goods* (Princeton, N.J.: Princeton University Press, 1971), pp. 112–14.

[23] Downturn points might alternatively be defined as those points at which the
incremental pivot contributions remain constant, or increase at a decreasing rate.
By this definition, these would be the points $(0, 1)$, $(1, 5)$, $(2, 5)$, and $(3, 5)$ in Figure
3.2, which do not qualify as downturn points by our more stringent original definition.

[24] Even though there is a drop from 0.17 to 0.14 in the incremental pivot contribu-

Empirical Thresholds. If the risk to an uncommitted member of not join-ing a dominant protocoalition at the final stage becomes progressively greater—and the benefits that the protocoalition leader should, and needs to, offer at the final stage correspondingly less—then we would expect to find empirical evidence that this kind of calculation underlies the forma-tion of coalitions in actual voting situations.[25] In fact, this appears to be the case for presidential and vice-presidential nominations in national party conventions, which we shall examine in greater detail later. For now we need only take note of the fact that in those conventions that have operated under majority rule, the final stage seems to be set when one candidate captures 42 per cent or more of the votes on a ballot, for no candidate has ever lost the nomination once he has gained more than 41 per cent of the votes on a ballot.[26]

A common explanation for take-off occurring at such a threshold is that "delegations wish to be on bandwagons because support of the nominee at the convention will be a basic criterion for the later distribu-

tion of an uncommitted member to Y as the process moves from cell $(0, 0)$ to $(0, 1)$ to $(0, 2)$, the increments then escalate again in value up to cell $(0, 5)$. This early drop-off in the incremental contribution between cells $(0, 1)$ and $(0, 2)$ is unique among the lattices considered and indicates the relatively greater value of a first commitment to a degenerate protocoalition than a second or third commitment in the combination case.

[25] Perhaps the same might be true in nonvoting situations as well. In tennis, for example, the decision rule for a set is that a player must take six games at least by a margin of two over his opponent or the set goes extra games until one player achieves a two-game lead over the other (similar to the rule for individual games). From in-formal observations, it seems that when the score in games is, say, 4–1, both players will fight harder to win the next game than when the score is 5–1, and the situation looks most promising for the winning player and nearly hopeless for the losing player, who must take six straight games to win at 7–5. If one interprets games as uncommitted members, gaining a "sufficient" number to achieve take-off at the next-to-last stage is often considered more crucial (i.e., worth more to the partici-pants) than persuading the decisive member to join (i.e., clinching the final game) at the last stage. Strategy is another sport, football, where the third down is usually considered more important than the fourth, might also be interpreted in these terms.

[26] Ulysses S. Grant just missed this threshold (which he set) when he polled 41 per cent of the votes on the 35th ballot of the 1880 Republican convention and went on to lose to James A. Garfield on the 36th ballot. In Democratic conventions prior to 1936, when the decision rule was two-thirds, the threshold based on past conven-tions is a figure exceeding 55 per cent; Martin Van Buren polled 55 per cent of the votes on the first ballot of the 1844 convention, with James K. Polk eventually emerging as the winner on the ninth ballot. See Richard C. Bain, *Convention Decisions and Voting Records* (Washington, D.C.: Brookings Institution, 1960), an indispen-sable sourcebook for voting data on most conventions; see also Thomas Hudson McKee, *The National Conventions and Platforms of all Political Parties, 1789–1905: Convention, Popular and Electoral Vote* (Baltimore: Friedenwald Co., 1906). The strong residual support commanded by both Grant and Van Buren might in part be a function of the fact that both had previously served as president but had not been reelected (Grant did not run for a third term in 1876) in the term prior to being re-jected by their parties.

tion of Presidential favors and patronage."[27] While this kind of calculation undoubtedly occurs, we would suggest that the bandwagon effect might be more closely tied to the actual voting process in conventions.[28] In particular, this mystical psychological force[29] that many have observed grips electors in the frenzy of political combat and sweeps the front-runner on to victory may have very strong roots in the kind of rational calculation of take-off and downturn points suggested by our models.[30] In attempting a scientific explanation of such a phenomenon, it is not useful to begin by relegating it to the realm of the supernatural and thereby rendering it incapable of explanation in terms of natural forces.

To be more precise, the empirical thresholds given above for national party conventions support the principle that there is a take-off point, prior to a protocoalition's achieving minimal winning size, that is probably followed by a downturn point of diminishing returns in payoffs to prospective members. This principle, applicable to the formation of

[27] Gerald Pomper, *Nominating the President: The Politics of Convention Choice* (Evanston, Ill.: Northwestern University Press, 1963), p. 144. See also Nelson W. Polsby and Aaron Wildavsky, *Presidential Elections: Strategies of American Electoral Politics*, 2d ed. (New York: Charles Scribner's Sons, 1968), pp. 97–103.

[28] Insofar as patronage depends on the stage when a winning coalition is joined in a convention, a calculation based on *post*election patronage is, of course, consistent with our calculation based on voting in conventions.

[29] "The bandwagon is a fever that takes statistics out of the definition of politics. It's a thing of chemistry that boils blood, jumps feet, waves hands, shouts voices, bangs fists, and heightens hangovers. It parts from reason in the same way that love does or hate does. It is a mass orgy of feeling that sweeps with the fervor of a religious revival. It is the Fourth of July on Christmas morning." Ralph G. Martin, *Ballots & Bandwagons* (Chicago: Rand McNally & Co., 1964), p. 444. The drama of the nomination process is highlighted in Herbert Eaton's *Presidential Timber: A History of Nominating Conventions, 1868–1960* (New York: Free Press of Glencoe, 1964), a personalized account that relies heavily on anecdotes and vignettes.

[30] This is not to say that electors actually *make* the complex calculations of our models but instead that they may somehow "sense" the *results* of the calculations with more or less clarity. While we have no data on the perceptions of electors that would substantiate this hypothesis, the thresholds do provide indirect evidence of behavior that is not inconsistent with the formal logic of the models, even if this logic does not capture whatever are the complex and subtle psychological determinants of the electors' choices. That the quantitative calculations are not a sufficient explanation, however, will become clear later; yet even the failures of our models serve the valuable heuristic function of suggesting what directions we might follow in developing more complete forms of explanation—instead of labeling something irrational and, *ipso facto*, inexplicable. For more on this point, see notes 53 and 57. For a general discussion and test of "rationality" in electoral politics, see William H. Riker and Peter C. Ordeshook, "A Theory of the Calculus of Voting," *American Political Science Review*, LXII (March, 1968), 25–42; and Michael J. Shapiro, "Rational Political Man: A Synthesis of Economic and Social-Psychological Perspectives," *ibid.*, LXVIII (Dec., 1969), 1106–19. A discussion of various meanings of "rationality" and an assessment of the extent to which behavior is "rational" in experimental games is given in William H. Riker and William J. Zavoina, "Rational Behavior in Politics: Evidence from a Three Person Game," *ibid.*, LXIX (March, 1970), 48–60.

protocoalitions, suggests an extension and refinement of the "size principle" previously advanced by Riker to explain the behavior of winning coalitions: as protocoalitions approach minimal winning size, they approach thresholds at which take-off occurs and it subsequently becomes irrational to bid increasingly more for new members, since victory can be attained with decreasing investments; once attained, the protocoalition becomes a winning coalition and can maintain its dominance over a long period of time only by paring off members who inflate it to greater than minimal winning size.[31] This illustrates well the kind of insights a theoretical model can offer the analyst in trying to account for observed, if somewhat mysterious, features of a political process.

To be sure, different assumptions will produce different thresholds when the value of joining the larger protocoalition, Y, exceeds the value of not joining (take-off occurs), or when the incremental value Y offers additional members for joining begins to decline (downturn occurs). There is a priori no "best" set of assumptions; the determination of the set most appropriate to particular situations must await empirical testing. Only when two protocoalitions of approximately equal size bid for the uncommitted members does it seem likely that the take-off and downturn points will be arrested to the very end and the price demanded by, and bids offered to, the uncommitted members will rise uninterruptedly because they will remain to the end decisive to both protocoalitions.[32]

In the next two sections we shall develop some probabilistic models that will provide us with another perspective on coalition-formation processes. The calculations for these models are based on a somewhat different set of assumptions than the pivot calculations, but they are fully interpretable within the previous framework of movements along the diagonals of a lattice. In the interest of economy, we shall present the probabilistic lattice calculations only for combinations (and without graphs) and not permutations, though for comparative purposes we shall summarize the dynamic suggested by the permutation calculations after first analyzing the lattices based on combinations. In each section we shall distinguish results based on calculations for minimal winning coalitions from those based on calculations for any winning coalitions.

---

[31] For an explication of the size principle, which is, strictly speaking, applicable only to social situations similar to *n*-person zero-sum games where side payments are allowed, whose players are rational, and where they have perfect information, see Riker, *The Theory of Political Coalitions*, pp. 32 ff.

[32] Cf. Coleman's calculation of a nondecreasing marginal expected utility to the actor gaining commitments at the same rate as his opponent. "The Marginal Utility of a Vote Commitment," *op. cit.*, pp. 48, 56.

Calculating the Probability of Being in a (Minimal) Winning Coalition

Minimal Winning Coalition. We shall now drop the notion of pivotalness used in the calculation of payoffs to members in Figures 3.1 and 3.2. Instead, we shall assume that the members of each protocoalition are always the first to commit themselves in the voting body and ask in how many ways the uncommitted members can be added to each protocoalition in order to make it minimal winning.[33] (Recall that no assumption about order of commitment was made in the pivotal models: an actor was pivotal only if he were essential to a coalition's remaining winning, regardless of when he joined.)

To illustrate this computation, consider lattice cell (1, 2) in Figure 3.4 for combinations. In order for the single member of the first protocoalition (X) to be a member of a minimal winning coalition, he must succeed in attracting five of the seven uncommitted members. There are $_7C_5 = 21$ ways in which this is possible, as there are $_7C_4 = 35$ possible ways in which the larger two-member protocoalition (Y) can attract the necessary four uncommitted members to become minimal winning.[34] If we assume that the $56 = 21 + 35$ ways in which both protocoalitions can become minimal winning are equally likely—that is, each uncommitted member is coolly independent and has no predisposition to side more frequently with some of his fellow uncommitteds than with others— then we can take the relative proportions of these combinations of five ($21/56 = 3/8 = 0.375$) and four ($35/56 = 5/8 = 0.625$) as the respective probabilities of the smaller and larger protocoalitions' becoming minimal winning.[35]

[33] For an elementary treatment of the counting and probabilistic concepts that follow, see John G. Kemeny, J. Laurie Snell, and Gerald L. Thompson, *Introduction to Finite Mathematics*, 2d ed. (Englewood Cliffs, N.J.: Prentice-Hall, 1966), chaps. 3 and 4. A description and applications of the Shapley-Shubik index are given on pp. 79–82, 113–15, *ibid.*

[34] Allowing for all possible arrangements, the number of permutations of five uncommitted members with X is $_7C_5 5!3! = 15,120$; of four uncommitted members with Y, $_7C_4 4!4! = 20,160$.

[35] Strictly speaking, these are conditional probabilities at each lattice cell, with the condition being that the process is at a particular cell. The probability of this condition's obtaining might be calculated from the relative proportion of times the distribution of X, Y, and uncommitted members at each cell would occur by chance, assuming that all different combinations of X, Y, and the uncommitted members, at each lattice cell, are equiprobable. We have not bothered to make this latter calculation since we are primarily interested in comparing X's chances with Y's, given that the process is at a particular lattice cell, and only secondarily in the unconditional probability that X (or Y) would be at a particular cell in the lattice *and* simultaneously go on to become minimal winning. This calculation is developed, however, in Steven J. Brams

Figure 3.4. Lattice of probabilities of being in a minimal winning coalition

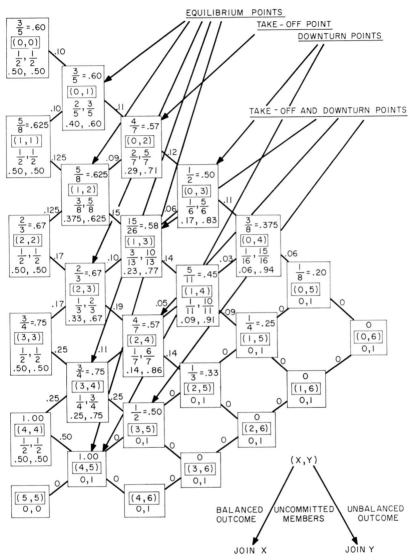

and John Heilman, "When to Join a Coalition, and with How Many Others, Depends on What You Expect the Outcome to Be" (paper presented at the Seminar on Mathematical Theory of Collective Decisions, Harbour Town, S.C., Aug. 8–14, 1971; and at the Annual Meeting of the American Political Science Association, Chicago, Sept. 7–11, 1971).

For all lattice cells in Figure 3.4, the complementary probabilities of each protocoalition's becoming minimal winning are given below the protocoalitions in each cell. Of course, when each of the two protocoalitions has the same number of members, each can attract the number of uncommitted members necessary to become minimal winning in the same number of ways. Since each of the tied protocoalitions in this case lays claim to the same number of points (combinations) in the probabilistic sample space, each has an equal probability (0.50) of eventually achieving minimal winning size. Even (unformed) protocoalitions of zero members at lattice cells (0, 0), (0, 1), (0, 2), (0, 3), and (0, 4) have some chance of eventually attracting the six uncommitted members necessary to become minimal winning, albeit this may be considered a degenerate case.

The "expected" probability that an uncommitted member will be a member of a minimal winning coalition, in alliance with one of the two protocoalitions, is given above each cell in Figure 3.4. To illustrate this computation of the mathematical expectation for lattice cell $(1, 2)$, note that $5/7$ of the seven uncommitted members are needed to form a minimal winning coalition with the smaller one-member protocoalition (X), and $4/7$ of the seven uncommitted members are needed to form a minimal winning coalition with the larger two-member protocoalition (Y). As given in Figure 3.4, the respective probabilities that X and Y will become minimal winning are $3/8$ and $5/8$. The *expected proportion* of the seven uncommitted members who will be in a minimal winning coalition is, therefore, the sum of the products of the proportions of uncommitted members necessary to form such a coalition ($5/7$ and $4/7$) and the respective probabilities that these protocoalitions will indeed become minimal winning ($3/8$ and $5/8$):

$$\left[\frac{5}{7} \cdot \frac{3}{8}\right] + \left[\frac{4}{7} \cdot \frac{5}{8}\right] = \frac{5}{8}.$$

This expected proportion can be interpreted as the *expected probability* that a randomly selected uncommitted member will be a member of a minimal winning coalition, given that such a coalition forms which includes one of the two opposing protocoalitions.

This probabilistic calculation for minimal winning coalitions suggests a dynamic not unlike that which we observed in the calculation of the proportion of pivots for the two protocoalitions and uncommitted members. The probabilities that members of the larger protocoalition (Y) will be in a minimal winning coalition for lattice cells (0, 1), (1, 2), (2, 3), (3, 4), and (4, 5) are identical to the expected probabilities that an uncommitted member will be in a minimal winning coalition, indicating that a one-member disparity between the two protocoalitions is a point of equilibrium (or indifference) for the uncommitted member who considers joining the larger protocoalition. To the left and above these points in the lattice, when the protocoalitions are tied, it always pays for the un-committed member to remain uncommitted; to the right and below these points, when the disparity between the two protocoalitions is greater than one member, it pays for the uncommitted member to join Y (except at cell (4, 6), where Y is already winning), producing take-off and the movement of the process toward an unbalanced outcome.[36]

This dynamic toward an unbalanced outcome can be understood from the numbers given along the lines connecting the lattice cells in Figure 3.4. These indicate the amount by which the uncommitted member can raise the probability that each of the protocoalitions will become minimal winning by joining either X (moving the process diagonally downward and to the left) or Y (moving the process diagonally downward and to the right). The increment in the probability of becoming minimal winning that the uncommitted member contributes by joining Y is always greater than the increment he generates for X, except when Y has five members (i.e., is blocking) and the uncommitted member contributes nothing to either X or Y.[37]

Presumably, if an uncommitted member's role in the affairs of a grow-ing protocoalition is proportional to the amount by which he increases its chances of achieving minimal winning size, it would always pay for an uncommitted member to join the larger protocoalition to maximize his future influence in its affairs. Thus, as previously (and with the same qualifications), the dynamic of this model is toward an unbalanced out-come.

As in the models based on pivot proportions, a drop in the contribu-tions (probabilistic here) of uncommitted members who join the larger protocoalition at downturn points (0, 3), (1, 3), (2, 4), and (3, 5) in

[36] "Take-off" could as reasonably be interpreted to occur at those points (e.g., cell (1, 2)) where the probability of Y's becoming minimal winning, when joined by an uncommitted member who moves the process toward an unbalanced outcome (e.g., at cell (1, 3)), is greater at cell (1, 3) (0.77) than an uncommitted member's previous expected probability of becoming minimal winning if he remained uncommitted at cell (1, 2) (0.625). So interpreted, these "take-off" points would be the "equilibrium" points in Figure 3.4 and tend to push the process toward an unbalanced outcome earlier.

[37] He contributes nothing because X's probability of becoming minimal winning is 0 and Y's probability is 1 (because we assume one protocoalition eventually wins and that can only be Y since defections are not allowed in the model). Thus, when an uncommitted member joins Y and changes it from a five-member blocking coalition to a six-member minimal winning coalition, he does nothing to alter X's certainty of eventually losing and Y's certainty of eventually winning.

Figure 3.4 [38] — as well as (4, 5), which is both a downturn and equilibrium point — may substantially lower the later bidding for uncommitted members. Curiously, when permutations are used in the calculation of the protocoalition probabilities, the incremental probabilities increase progressively up to the point at which Y has five members and is therefore blocking (i.e., the downturn points are (0, 5), (1, 5), (2, 5), (3, 5), and (4, 5)), though the take-off points remain the same as for combinations and the incremental probabilities again favor the larger protocoalition.

It is important to note that the expected probabilities associated with the uncommitted members at each lattice cell characterize in a strict sense only an uncommitted member who has been randomly selected. Unlike pivots, these probabilities are indivisible — and therefore public goods since they cannot be withheld from any of the uncommitted members — and it is impossible to say what each uncommitted member's share is. Therefore, we invent the fiction of a "randomly selected uncommitted member" so that we will have somebody to compare with the members of each protocoalition, each of whom derives the same benefits (in terms of the probability of winning) as all other members of his protocoalition do.

Any Winning Coalition. The calculation of the probabilities that each protocoalition will become winning with not only six but possibly seven, eight, nine, or ten members — and the expected probability that a randomly selected uncommitted member will be included in such a winning coalition — is somewhat more complicated than, though completely analogous to, the calculation for the minimal winning case. Again, for purposes of illustration, consider lattice cell (1, 2). The one-member protocoalition (X) can become winning by picking up five, six, or all seven of the uncommitted members in

$$\binom{7}{5} + \binom{7}{6} + \binom{7}{7} = 21 + 7 + 1 = 29 \text{ ways,}$$

and the two-member protocoalition (Y) can become winning by picking up four, five, six, or all seven of the uncommitted members in

$$\binom{7}{4} + \binom{7}{5} + \binom{7}{6} + \binom{7}{7} = 35 + 21 + 7 + 1 = 64 \text{ ways.}$$

[38] Unlike the previous pivot models, where the downturn points always followed the take-off points, these downturn points (except for the degenerate case at cell (0, 3)) are coincident with the take-off points. Those empirical situations where an observed bandwagon and underdog effect develop simultaneously would tend to lend credence to this model.

The probabilities of X and Y's becoming any winning, therefore, are respectively $29/93 = 0.31$ and $64/93 = 0.69$, as shown in Figure 3.5.

The expected probability that a randomly selected uncommitted member will be in an any winning coalition is the sum of the product of the proportion of uncommitted members in all winning coalitions ($5/6$, $6/7$, and $7/7$ for X; $4/7$, $5/7$, $6/7$, and $7/7$ for Y) and the respective probabilities of X's winning with six, seven, or eight members and Y's winning with seven, eight, or nine members:

$$\left[\frac{5}{7}\cdot\frac{21}{93} + \frac{6}{7}\cdot\frac{7}{93} + \frac{7}{7}\cdot\frac{1}{93}\right] + \left[\frac{4}{7}\cdot\frac{35}{93} + \frac{5}{7}\cdot\frac{21}{93} + \frac{6}{7}\cdot\frac{7}{93} + \frac{7}{7}\cdot\frac{1}{93}\right] = \frac{64}{93}$$

$$= 0.69.$$

This expected probability that an uncommitted member will be in an any winning coalition is greater than the comparable probability of his being in a minimal winning coalition (0.625) given at cell (1, 2) in Figure 3.4. The inflation of the expected probabilities for the uncommitted members is matched, however, by the inflation of the probabilities of Y's winning and a corresponding deflation of the complementary probabilities of X's winning. In fact, the equilibrium points, which separate the take-off points from the points where it pays for the uncommitted members to remain uncommitted, are the same in Figure 3.5 as those in the minimal winning case given in Figure 3.4. Unlike Figure 3.4, however, where most of the downturn points are coincident with the take-off points, downturn points (1, 2), (2, 3), (3, 4) and (4, 5) in Figure 3.5 actually precede the take-off points (they are coincident with the equilibrium points), suggesting the presence of an underdog effect prior to a bandwagon effect. As a possible illustration of this sequence, some of John F. Kennedy's support in the 1960 presidential campaign may well have been attributable to the underdog effect prior to his television debates with Richard M. Nixon, the bandwagon effect taking hold after the debates. The precise conditions under which the predictions of this model are upheld, however, must await more systematic kinds of evidence. (When permutations are used, this model predicts *simultaneous* take-off and downturn points, as in the minimal winning case for combinations [Figure 3.4].)

There is an important difference between the relative magnitude of the incremental probabilities given along the diagonal lines of the lattice in Figure 3.5 and those of previous lattices. In all previous models, the larger protocoalition was favored, but in Figure 3.5 the incremental probabilities reveal that an uncommitted member can make a greater probabilistic contribution to the smaller protocoalition (X). If the uncom-

Figure 3.5.   Lattice of probabilities of being in any winning coalition

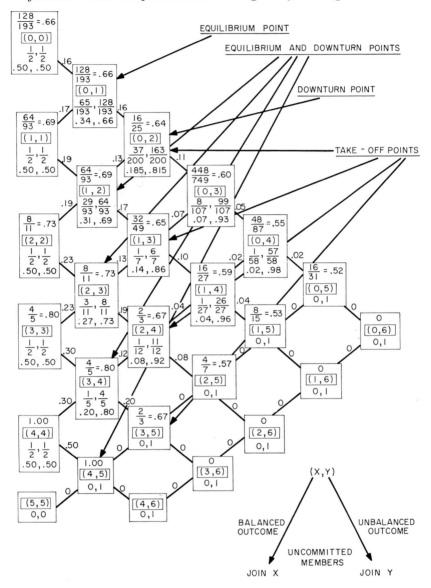

mitted member's goal is to maximize his incremental contribution to the probability that one of the two protocoalitions will become winning, he can best achieve this goal by casting his lot with X and thus pushing the process toward a balanced outcome.

Methodological Digression. We can perhaps give some insight into the differences in these incremental probabilities for the minimal winning and any winning cases by comparing them with a similar concept defined by James S. Coleman, "the increment in probability of passage due to a vote commitment." [39] When passage for a measure requires k additional votes from the n uncommitted members $(k \leq n)$, Coleman's incremental probability is equal to the probability of obtaining $(k - 1)$ votes from $(n - 1)$ uncommitted members times the difference in the probability of passage with a commitment (1.00) and without (0.50). Instead of assuming that uncommitted members choose for or against passage (in our terms, join one protocoalition or the other) with probability equal to 0.50, we have assumed that all combinations of the uncommitted members necessary to form a minimal winning or any winning coalition with one protocoalition or the other are equiprobable.

These assumptions differ only in their definitions of sample spaces of points representing equally likely outcomes. If, for example, in the Coleman model the larger protocoalition, Y, is for passage at lattice cell $(3, 4)$, the number of ways in which Y can obtain $k - 1$ $(= 1)$ votes from $n - 1$ $(= 2)$ uncommitted members—and so make the nth (3d) uncommitted member decisive for passage—is

$$\binom{2}{1} = 2,$$ representing outcome $(4, 5)$—i.e., there are two ways in which one of two uncommitted members can join X and the other Y and still leave the third uncommitted member crucial to Y's winning.

But there are also two ways in which this third uncommitted member would play no part in the passage of the measure:

$$\binom{2}{2} = 1,$$ representing outcome $(3, 6)$—i.e., there is one way in which two uncommitted members can join Y;

$$\binom{2}{0} = 1,$$ representing outcome $(5, 4)$—i.e., there is one way in which two uncommitted members can join X.

Therefore, the probability is $2/4 = 1/2$ that one vote commitment will make a difference in passage, and the increment in probability of passage with as opposed to without a vote commitment (probability 1.00 versus 0.50) is

$$\left(1 - \frac{1}{2}\right) \left(\frac{1}{2}\right) = \frac{1}{4}.$$

[39] "The Marginal Utility of a Vote Commitment," *op. cit.*, p. 45.

Instead of considering sample spaces of outcomes with one (or more) members uncommitted, our calculations are based on sample spaces of outcomes in which we assume all uncommitted members eventually join one protocoalition or the other. As a basis for comparison with the Coleman model, consider the following three models. From any lattice cell (X, Y),

1. when ties are permitted, all outcomes (X', Y') are possible where $(X' \geq X, Y' \geq Y)$ and $X' + Y' =$ total number of members in the voting body;
2. when ties are not permitted (our previous "any winning" model), $X' = Y'$ outcomes are impossible events; and
3. when only minimal winning coalitions are permitted, $X' = Y'$ as well as $\mid X' - Y' \mid > 2$ for even-numbered bodies, and $\mid X' - Y' \mid > 1$ for odd-numbered bodies, are impossible events.

To illustrate the differences in the calculation of incremental probabilities between these three models and the Coleman model, consider again the movement of the process from lattice cell $(3, 4)$ to cell $(3, 5)$. At cell $(3, 4)$, the commitment of an uncommitted member to the larger protocoalition moves the process to cell $(3, 5)$, from whence it could terminate at outcomes $(5, 5)$, $(4, 6)$, or $(3, 7)$, depending on which of the two protocoalitions $(X$ or $Y)$ each of the two uncommitted members joins after the process reaches cell $(3, 5)$. These outcomes, with the numbers of ways in which each can occur for the any winning (ties permitted), any winning (ties not permitted), and minimal winning calculations, are given in Table 3.1, along with the designation of whether each outcome is favorable (F) or unfavorable (U) to passage, assuming the larger protocoalition, Y, is for passage.

Table 3.1.   Possible outcomes for three models at cell $(3, 5)$

Outcomes	Number of ways in which outcomes can occur		
	Any winning (ties permitted)	Any winning (ties not permitted)	Minimal winning
$(5, 5)$	$\binom{2}{2} = 1$ (U)	Impossible	Impossible
$(4, 6)$	$\binom{2}{1} = 2$ (F)	2 (F)	2 (F)
$(3, 7)$	$\binom{2}{0} = 1$ (F)	1 (F)	Impossible
Total	4	3	2

Table 3.2. Possible outcomes for three models at cell (3, 4)

Outcomes	Number of ways in which outcomes can occur		
	Any winning (ties permitted)	Any winning (ties not permitted)	Minimal winning
(6, 4)	$\binom{3}{3} = 1$ (U)	1 (U)	1 (U)
(5, 5)	$\binom{3}{2} = 3$ (U)	Impossible	Impossible
(4, 6)	$\binom{3}{1} = 3$ (F)	3 (F)	3 (F)
(3, 7)	$\binom{3}{0} = 1$ (F)	1 (F)	Impossible
Total	8	5	4

At lattice cell (3, 4) *prior* to the commitment of an uncommitted member to Y, the possible outcomes and the number of ways in which they can occur are given in Table 3.2. Comparing Tables 3.1 and 3.2, we see that as the process moves from lattice cell (3, 4) in Table 3.2 to cell (3, 5) in Table 3.1, the proportion of outcomes in which Y wins increases from $4/8$ to $3/4$ (0.25 increment) for the any winning (ties permitted) model, from $4/5$ to $3/3$ (0.20 increment) for the any winning (ties not permitted) model (see Figure 3.5), and from $3/4$ to $2/2$ (0.25 increment) for the minimal winning model (see Figure 3.4).

Except for our any winning model where ties are not permitted, Coleman's calculations and ours produce the same incremental probability (0.25) for the above example, though the different assumptions of the different models may produce greater deviations in the incremental probabilities for other lattice cells. Which of the models is best is largely a question of the empirical situation one wishes to study and, in particular, what one envisages as the possible outcomes. Our models did not allow, for example, the outcome (3, 6), with one member remaining uncommitted, but in a particular situation this outcome might represent a more feasible possibility than the very lopsided outcome (3, 7), which two of our models allowed. The most appropriate model is the one whose sample space of outcomes best reflects the actual outcomes possible in a voting body. Moreover, if there were sufficient information to weight the possible outcomes, then particular outcomes could be assigned more sample points than others commensurate with their greater a priori probabilities of occurrence.

Since the only difference between our any winning model with ties and that without ties is that the latter assumes that one protocoalition eventually wins and the (5, 5) blocking option is impossible, these two models are identical for voting bodies with an odd number of members and majority rule; all blocking coalitions are winning coalitions in such a body. Only when the decision rule requires more than a simple majority does it seem likely that blocking strategies will differ significantly from winning strategies and therefore be worthy of separate consideration. In voting bodies where members envisage outcomes as close, the exclusion by the minimal winning model of all outcomes except those involving (in bodies of odd size) one-vote or (in bodies of even size) two-vote margins may be appropriate in the calculation of the probabilities. Still another model might permit both blocking and minimal winning outcomes in bodies of even size. Whatever model one chooses as appropriate to a particular situation, its implications for coalition-building processes may be explored in the manner described above.[40]

Expected Share of Spoils. Previously we showed that the incremental probabilities based on being in an any winning coalition, given in Figure 3.5, favor an uncommitted member's joining the smaller protocoalition, X. We shall now show that it may not always be in the best interest of an uncommitted member to maximize his incremental contribution by joining X, especially when X's chances of becoming winning appear dim even with the support of the uncommitted member. Should an uncommitted member at lattice cell (2, 4) in Figure 3.5, for example, prefer to increase by 0.12 X's probability of winning to an unspectacular one chance in five when he could raise by a somewhat smaller increment (0.08) Y's probability of winning to an unbeatable 1.00? Perhaps he might, but undoubtedly some uncommitted members may reason in this case that it would be better to insure against losing by making the larger protocoalition a blocking coalition with five members than to be promised a slightly larger share of the eventual spoils but accept a much greater risk of losing and never realizing them.

We can formalize the above notion by calculating the *expected share of spoils* of an uncommitted member. This share will be equal to the probability, p, that a protocoalition will win if an uncommitted member joins, times the incremental contribution, c, of the uncommitted member to this probability.[41] Thus, at cell (2, 4) in Figure 3.5, if the uncommitted mem-

---

[40] We should point out that Coleman's interest in *ibid.* was more in the marginal utility analysis of collective decisions than in coalition-formation processes, which is perhaps one reason he did not choose to explore the implications of defining different sample spaces of possible outcomes.

[41] A similar utility calculation is suggested in Frohlich, Oppenheimer, and Young, *op. cit.*, p. 89. See also Anthony Downs, *An Economic Theory of Democracy* (New York: Harper and Row, 1957), pp. 47–50, 159.

ber joins the smaller protocoalition (X), he moves the process to cell $(3, 4)$ where X has a $p = 0.20$ chance of winning. Furthermore, his incremental contribution to the probability that X will win at cell $(3, 4)$ is $c = 0.12$. Hence, if the uncommitted member joins X, his expected share of spoils is $(0.20)(0.12) = 0.024$. If, on the other hand, he joins Y and moves the process from cell $(2, 4)$ to cell $(2, 5)$, the probability that Y will win at cell $(2, 5)$ is 1.00 and his incremental contribution is 0.08. Hence, his expected share of spoils is $(1.00)(0.08) = 0.08$. Thus, while an uncommitted member's incremental contribution to the probability that Y will win is less than his incremental contribution to the probability that X will win (0.08 versus 0.12), his expected share of spoils, a function not only of his incremental contribution but also of the probability of choosing a winner, is enhanced by joining Y rather than X (0.08 versus 0.024).

This calculation of an uncommitted member's expected share of spoils vitiates the attractiveness that the smaller protocoalition would have for the uncommitted member who seeks to maximize his role in a potential winning coalition. Yet, even when the potential for winning is probabilistically small, support for a smaller protocoalition on the part of some uncommitted members might prove rational in the sense of providing a sufficient psychological impetus to dampen a quick take-off on the part of the larger protocoalition. Support for the smaller protocoalition might also prove rational if an uncommitted member, for any variety of reasons, feels he has no hope of influencing the policies or actions of the larger protocoalition, even if he calculates that that protocoalition is the probable winner.[42]

Patently, many political processes tend toward a balanced outcome, and as we shall see in our empirical example later, the inability of our models to account for this directly may lie in part in the fact that the forces driving the process toward take-off at an early stage, suggested by some of our abstract rational calculations, may not become evident to the actors involved until a much later stage. As we saw earlier, however, the underdog effect, considered as a countervailing force to the bandwagon effect, may be a very rational response on the part of uncommitted members to the reduced payoffs offered at a downturn point by the larger protocoalition.

Summary. The probabilities that each protocoalition will be in a minimal winning or any winning coalition are based on the number of different ways each protocoalition can attract different combinations (or permutations) of uncommitted members in order to reach (minimal or any) win-

---

[42] See Nelson Polsby, "Decision-Making at the National Conventions," *Western Political Quarterly*, XIII (Sept., 1960), 617, Proposition 5.

ning size. For the uncommitted members, the expected probability of being in a (minimal or any) winning coalition is based on both the probability that each protocoalition will become (minimal or any) winning and the proportion of previously uncommitted members who would be so included in each coalition, given that one protocoalition or the other is eventually victorious. We showed that the minimal winning and any winning models differed from Coleman's only in their specification of different sample spaces of equiprobable outcomes.

In the minimal winning case, an uncommitted member's incremental contribution to the probability that the larger protocoalition (Y) will become minimal winning is always greater than his incremental contribution to the probability that the smaller protocoalition (X) will become minimal winning. When all winning coalitions are taken into account in the calculations, however, the incremental contribution of the uncommitted member to X is greater, reversing the dynamic from favoring an unbalanced to favoring a balanced outcome. (This is not true for incremental probabilities based on permutations, which favor Y in both the minimal winning and any winning cases.) Yet this apparent divergence in outcomes predicted in the minimal winning and any winning cases for combinations is blurred in the any winning case by the consideration of the expected share of spoils that would accrue to the uncommitted member who joins X rather than Y. Since an uncommitted member can expect a greater share of spoils by joining Y, the dynamic inhering in both probabilistic models would seem to push the outcome toward one of imbalance. But because most of the downturn points are coincident with the take-off points in the minimal winning model, and precede the take-off points in the any winning model, we would expect that an underdog effect might tend to offset this dynamic. Indeed, the empirical data we shall present later suggests a marked delay in the realization of take-off.

Calculating the Total Probabilistic Payoff

Minimal Winning Coalition. The lattices in Figures 3.4 and 3.5 suggest a basically similar dynamic at work for the calculation of probabilities based on both the minimal winning and any winning models. When we sum the payoffs in probabilities for all members—both those members committed to one of the two protocoalitions and those uncommitted—we get a somewhat different perspective on the dynamics of coalition-formation processes.

To illustrate the total payoff calculation, consider lattice cell $(1, 2)$ in the minimal winning case (Figure 3.4). The total payoff to the single member of the smaller protocoalition is (1) (3/8) = 3/8; to the two members of the larger protocoalition, (2) (5/8) = 10/8; and to the seven uncommitted members, (7) (5/8) = 35/8. For all ten members of the body, the sum of these payoffs is

$$\frac{3}{8} + \frac{10}{8} + \frac{35}{8} = \frac{48}{8} = 6,$$

which is also the sum of payoffs for all the other lattice cells in the minimal winning cases (as well as being the decision rule of the body). To show this, assume as before that

X = number of members in first protocoalition,
Y = number of members in second protocoalition.

Then

$6 - X$ = number of additional members necessary for X to be minimal winning,
$6 - Y$ = number of additional members necessary for Y to be minimal winning,
$10 - X - Y$ = number of uncommitted members.

The sum of the probabilistic payoffs will be equal to the number of members committed to each protocoalition and the number uncommitted (X, Y, and $10 - X - Y$) times the respective probabilities that members of each of these subsets will be in a minimal winning coalition:

$$X\left[\frac{\binom{10-X-Y}{6-X}}{\binom{10-X-Y}{6-X} + \binom{10-X-Y}{6-Y}}\right]$$

$$+ Y\left[\frac{\binom{10-X-Y}{6-Y}}{\binom{10-X-Y}{6-X} + \binom{10-X-Y}{6-Y}}\right]$$

$$+ [10-X-Y]\left[\frac{\binom{10-X-Y}{6-X}\left[\frac{6-X}{10-X-Y}\right]}{\binom{10-X-Y}{6-X}}\right.$$

$$\left. + \frac{\binom{10-X-Y}{6-Y}\left[\frac{6-Y}{10-X-Y}\right]}{\binom{10-X-Y}{6-Y}}\right]$$

$$= \frac{[X + 6 - X]\begin{pmatrix} 10 - X - Y \\ 6 - X \end{pmatrix} + [Y + 6 - Y]\begin{pmatrix} 10 - X - Y \\ 6 - Y \end{pmatrix}}{\begin{pmatrix} 10 - X - Y \\ 6 - X \end{pmatrix} + \begin{pmatrix} 10 - X - Y \\ 6 - Y \end{pmatrix}} = 6.$$

For minimal winning coalitions, then, the sum of the probabilities for all members, which we shall call the *total probabilistic payoff* (which, of course, is *not* a probability measure), does not depend on how many members are committed to X and Y and how many are uncommitted: on balance, what is lost by some members is gained by other members when the coalition-formation process moves to a different lattice cell.

Any Winning Coalition. A balancing of losses and gains does not occur, however, when the calculation of the total probabilistic payoff is based on the any winning coalition model. For example, the calculation for lattice cell (1, 2) in Figure 3.5 is

$$(1)\begin{pmatrix} 29 \\ 93 \end{pmatrix} + (2)\begin{pmatrix} 64 \\ 93 \end{pmatrix} + (7)\begin{pmatrix} 64 \\ 93 \end{pmatrix} = \frac{605}{93} = 6.50.$$

For cell (1, 3), on the other hand, we get

$$(1)\begin{pmatrix} 1 \\ 7 \end{pmatrix} + (3)\begin{pmatrix} 6 \\ 7 \end{pmatrix} + (6)\begin{pmatrix} 32 \\ 49 \end{pmatrix} = \frac{325}{49} = 6.64.$$

In general, the payoffs are greater than the constant 6.00 value we computed above for cells in the minimal winning lattice (Figure 3.4).

The reason for the inflation of the 6.00 value can be seen from the fact that all the probability values in the any winning coalition lattice (Figure 3.5) are less for X, and greater for Y and the uncommitted members, than in the minimal winning coalition lattice (Figure 3.4). Since the increased contribution to the total probabilistic payoff from Y and the uncommitted members more than offsets the decreased contribution from X, this payoff will be greater than 6.00, except for lattice cells (4, 4) and (4, 5) and those cells in which Y has become a minimal winning coalition with the addition of a sixth member. In these cases, the probability values for the cells are identical in Figures 3.4 and 3.5, and so therefore are the total probabilistic payoffs of 6.00.

The total probabilistic payoffs for all protocoalition lattice cells in Figure 3.5 are given in Table 3.3 and show that the payoffs are equal when the protocoalitions are tied or one protocoalition has one more member than the other. Otherwise, when the number of members in X (moving across a row) is held constant, the total probabilistic payoff increases as the disparity in membership between the two protocoalitions increases; when the number of members in Y (moving up a column) is held constant, the total probabilistic payoff again increases as the disparity in membership between the two protocoalitions increases. Together, these tendencies push the outcome toward lattice cell $(0, 5)$, where the disparity between the two protocoalitions is maximal and the total probabilistic payoff is the greatest.

A major caveat must be stated concerning this conclusion, however. In the minimal winning case, the total probabilistic payoff of 6.00 arises simply as the sum over all ten members of the probability of being in a set (i.e., minimal winning coalition) always consisting of six members; so

Table 3.3. Total probabilistic payoffs for protocoalition lattice cells in Figure 3.5

Number of members in first protocoalition (X)	Number of members in second protocoalition (Y)					
	0	1	2	3	4	5
0	6.63	6.63	6.74	6.96	7.24	7.58
1		6.50	6.50	6.64	6.97	7.13
2			6.36	6.36	6.50	6.72
3				6.20	6.20	6.33
4					6.00	6.00

this sum of probabilities must always be 6.00. When the number in a winning coalition is allowed to be larger than six, the total probabilistic payoff will necessarily be equal to or greater than 6.00. Strictly speaking, the total probabilistic payoff is not a "payoff" in the game-theoretic sense, which is always equal to 1.00 and would in our examples be split up among just six, or six or more, members. The generally greater total probabilistic payoffs in the any winning coalition case express quantitatively the fact that more members on the average may be in a winning coalition, though, of course, each member's share might be correspondingly less and thereby negate any tendency for the outcome to move toward lattice cell $(0, 5)$, where it is possible for all members eventually to be on the winning side, i.e., at cell $(0, 10)$.

Summary. The total probabilistic payoff is computed by summing the probabilities that all members, either committed to one of the two protocoalitions or uncommitted, will be in a minimal winning or any winning coalition. In the minimal winning case, these expected payoffs are constant, and equal to the decision rule, for all lattice cells; so this calculation suggests no dynamic pushing the process toward any particular outcome.

When the calculation of the total probabilistic payoff is based on an *any winning* coalition, on the other hand, the payoff is no longer constant for all lattice cells but instead assumes its greatest value when the disparity between the size of the two protocoalitions is greatest. This second calculation suggests a dynamic tending to push the process toward an unbalanced outcome, although we noted that this dynamic might be throttled by the smaller share accruing to each member in the any winning coalition case. These conclusions hold without exception when the calculation of the total probabilistic payoffs is based on permutations rather than combinations.

Predicting the Take-Off Point in National Party Conventions

National party conventions provide us with very useful data to test the predictive capacity of some of our models of coalition-formation dynamics. In conventions with multiballot presidential and vice-presidential nominations, in particular, we can observe the shifting of protocoalitions from roll call to roll call as each candidate tries to accumulate the number of votes necessary for nomination, or perhaps the number necessary to block another candidate. As John McDonald put it, "The political conventions . . . are coalition games. Each candidate goes in generally with a number of votes short of a nominating majority. The 'game' is for each candidate to secure that majority through coalitions with other-candidate groups and at the same time to break up or prevent competing coalitions." [43]

In order to apply our models to voting data in national party conventions, it is necessary first to select those conventions that most closely approximate the conditions of the models, i.e., conventions with voting situations in which there are two opposing protocoalitions, each vying for the votes of the uncommitted members. In trying to approximate these conditions, we have chosen for analysis presidential and vice-presidential

---

[43] *Strategy in Poker, Business and War* (New York: W. W. Norton, 1950), p. 116; we owe this citation to William A. Gamson, "Coalition Formation at Presidential Nominating Conventions," *American Journal of Sociology*, LXVIII (Sept., 1962), 157. Using such attributes of candidates as their personal characteristics, fame, interest-group support, electoral record, ideological orientation, and the size and party composition of states from which they came — as well as the proportion of votes each received on convention ballots — Gamson predicts (or more accurately, retrodicts) with reasonable accuracy those coalitions of candidates that formed in several conventions since 1900. By contrast, we shall not attempt to retrodict the *composition* of coalitions using many behavioral variables but instead to show regularities in the *formation* of coalitions by analyzing only the distribution of votes on the final ballots.

balloting in *all* national party conventions (which began with the 1832 campaign) that met the following criteria: [44]

1. There were at least three ballots, or two ballots followed by a shift in the second ballot (counted as the third ballot) which assured the nomination for one candidate. The provision for at least three ballots allows us to distinguish the next-to-last stage (second-to-last ballot) from the last stage (next-to-last ballot) in the coalition process prior to nomination (last ballot).
2. On the second-to-last and next-to-last ballots, the first-place and second-place candidates occupied the same relative positions. We thus rule out those few nominations in which a "dark-horse" candidate shot up in the final balloting, which is likely to be an event that occurs at an unpredictable time after a period of deadlock.
3. The two leading candidates on the second-to-last and next-to-last ballots had more than 50 per cent of the votes, and no other candidate had 25 per cent or more of the votes. Further, the votes of all other candidates, together with the votes of *either* leading candidate, were sufficient for the nomination of each leading candidate.[45] By these criteria, we restrict our analysis to those conventions in which there are only two serious contenders, each capable of winning with the votes of the minor candidates, in order that we might determine if there is a take-off point prior to nomination where the leading candidate captured enough of the votes previously committed to minor candidates and favorite sons to insure his nomination on the next ballot.

Multiballot presidential nominations in three conventions (1948 Republican, 1884 Republican, and 1848 Whig) and the vice-presidential nomination in one convention (1844 Whig) met the above criteria, and the voting in these conventions for the two leading candidates, and all others together, on the three final ballots is shown in Table 3.4.[46] The

[44] Since our evidence is not simply anecdotal but based on *all* instances of nomination that satisfy the specified criteria, our conclusions pertain to a whole class of events and not just some that happen to fit the theory but whose criteria for inclusion cannot be specified.

[45] This eliminates all Democratic conventions prior to 1936, in which two-thirds of the votes were required for nomination. In the final stages of these conventions, typically the second-leading candidate, even with the votes of all minor candidates, could not muster the two-thirds necessary for nomination; in a few conventions, this was true for both leading candidates, making necessary a shift in votes from one leading candidate to the other to allow for the nomination of one.

[46] Contrary to our findings for these conventions that the largest protocoalition eventually triumphs, experimental studies of convention-type situations have shown

Table 3.4.   Voting in four conventions on three final ballots

Convention	Decision rule	Three final ballots	Candidates	Second to-last ballot	Next-to-last ballot	Last ballot
1948 Republican	548/1,094	1st–3d	Dewey	434	515	1,094
			Taft	224	274	0
			Other	436	305	0
1884 Republican	411/820	2d–4th	Blaine	349	375	541
			Arthur	276	274	207
			Other	195	171	72
1848 Whig	141/280	2d–4th	Taylor	118	133	171
			Clay	86	74	32
			Other	76	73	77
1844 Whig (VP)	138/275	1st–3d	Frelinghuysen	101	118	154
			Davis	83	75	79
			Other	91	82	42

Source: Data from Bain, *Convention Decisions and Voting Records*, Appendix D.

probabilities that the leading candidate in each of the four nominations could offer those "other" delegates, not committed to himself or the second-leading candidate (these "other" delegates surely might have had preferences for one or the other of the candidates, but we have no data on such preferences), of being in a minimal winning coalition are shown for the second-to-last and next-to-last ballots in Table 3.5, assuming all combinations of the delegates committed to minor candidates, and necessary for the leading candidates to attract to achieve bare majorities, are equally likely. For example, on the second-to-last ballot of the 1948 Republican convention, the number of ways that Dewey could get 114 of the 436 "other" delegates necessary to win is $_{436}C_{114}$; for Taft the number is $_{436}C_{324}$. Assuming these ways of eventually putting together a

a tendency of coalitions to form which exclude the largest protocoalition. This divergence in findings, however, seems largely due to the rather different initial conditions assumed in the experimental studies (three factions in a single-choice situation) and those that existed in the conventions studies here (in effect, two factions [protocoalitions] and a set of uncommitted members not acting as a cohesive voting bloc in a situation allowing for on-going choices [ballots]). For a review of the experimental studies, see Lawrence H. Nitz and James L. Phillips, "The Effects of Divisibility of Payoff on Confederative Behavior," *Journal of Conflict Resolution*, XIII (Sept., 1969), 381–87; see also William H. Riker, "Bargaining in a Three-Person Game," *American Political Science Review*, LXI (Sept., 1967), 642–56. On the role of neutral (or uncommitted) actors in coalition-building games, see Robert C. Ziller, Harmon Zeigler, Gary L. Gregor, and Wayne Peak, "The Neutral in a Communication Network under Conditions of Conflict," *American Behavioral Scientist*, XIII (Nov.–Dec., 1969), 265–82.

Table 3.5. Probabilities of "other" delegates being in a minimal winning coalition

Convention	Probability which leading candidate can offer "other" delegates of being in a minimal winning coalition		Expected probability of "other" delegates being in a minimal winning coalition	
	Second-to-last ballot	Next-to-last ballot	Second-to-last ballot	Next-to-last ballot
1948 Republican	.89	.99	.31	.12
1884 Republican	.83	.94	.38	.25
1848 Whig	.80	.99	.41	.12
1844 Whig (VP)	.69	.91	.47	.29
Mean	.80	.96	.39	.20

minimal winning coalition are equally likely for both candidates, Dewey's probability is, therefore,

$$\frac{\binom{436}{114}}{\binom{436}{114} + \binom{436}{324}} = \frac{(323)(324)}{(323)(324) + (114)(113)} = 0.89,$$

and Taft's complementary probability is 0.11.[47] Since $114/434 = 0.26$ of the "other" delegates would be in a minimal winning coalition with Dewey, and $324/434 = 0.74$ with Taft, the expected probability that a randomly selected "other" delegate will be in a minimal winning coalition (i.e., the proportion of "other" delegates in a minimal winning coalition with each candidate times the probability that that candidate will become minimal winning) is

$$(0.26)\ (0.89) + (0.74)\ (0.11) = 0.31.$$

It is remarkable that all the values of the probability that the leading candidate can offer "other" delegates of being in a minimal winning

[47] Dewey's probability would be higher, and Taft's lower, if the calculations were based on each candidate's being in an any winning coalition, but the conclusions that follow would not be affected. Neither would Dewey's preponderant advantage be very much cut if the pivot proportion model were used, since Dewey's proportion of pivots would be greater than Taft's by the same factor (approximately nine to one) that Dewey's probability of being in an any winning coalition is greater than Taft's probability. Even though Dewey has almost twice as many delegates sharing his pivots as Taft does, therefore, each Dewey delegate would on the average have significantly (almost five times!) more pivots than each Taft delegate.

coalition on the second-to-last ballot (range: 0.69 to 0.89) are less than all values on the last ballot (range: 0.91 to 0.99), suggesting the empirical generalization that take-off is achieved (i.e., the next ballot will be decisive, which we take as an operational definition of the point when take-off occurs) at a probability greater than 0.90; below 0.90, the momentum of the leading candidate falls short of sweeping him to victory on the next ballot. For the expected probability that "other" delegates will be in a minimal winning coalition, a similar empirical dividing line separates the second-to-last ballots (range: 0.47 to 0.31) from the next-to-last ballots (range: 0.29 to 0.12), with take-off occurring for values greater than 0.30 and not occurring for values less than 0.30. Not only, then, can we retrodict (i.e., predict a past state of affairs) the eventual winner in majority-rule conventions from the 42 per cent threshold, but, for a subset of nominations in these conventions, our models allow us to retrodict the ballot on which he will win from the vote distribution on the previous ballot.

For both calculations, the probability of four values falling in one class, coincident with the next-to-last ballot, and four in another class, coincident with the second-to-last ballot, is $4!4!/8! = 1/70 = 0.014$, which is small enough to establish that it is very unlikely that this result could have occurred by chance.[48] On the other hand, using the percentage of the total vote obtained by the leading candidate proves to be an unreliable guide: these percentages ranged from 37 (Frelinghuysen in the 1844 Whig convention) to 43 (Blaine in the 1844 Republican convention) on the second-to last ballots, 43 (Frelinghuysen in the 1844 Whig convention) to 48 (Taylor in the 1848 Whig convention) on the next-to-last ballots, with the 43 per cent received by Blaine on the second-to-last ballot of the 1844 Republican presidential nomination and by Frelinghuysen on the next-to-last ballot of the 1844 Whig vice-presidential nomination not providing us with a clear-cut demarcation between voting on the second-to-last and next-to-last ballots.

What does the application of this model reveal about the "rationality" of the "other" delegates' withholding their votes from the leading candidate on these near-final ballots? On the second-to-last ballot, the mean probability (see Table 3.5) that the leading candidate can offer the "other" delegates of being in a minimal winning coalition (0.80) is more than twice as great as the mean expected probability of their being in a minimal winning coalition (0.39). On the next-to-last ballot this disparity

---

[48] More precisely, if the $_8C_4 = 8!/4!4! = 70$ ways of choosing two subsets containing four elements each from a set of eight elements (four nominations, two ballots considered on each) are considered equally likely, then the probability of choosing that one way which partions the elements into those four occurring on the second-to-last ballot in each election and those four occurring on the next-to-last ballot in each election is 1/70.

jumps nearly to a factor of five (0.96 versus 0.20). Clearly, by this calculation delegates not committed to either of the two leading candidates hold out well beyond the point when it becomes rational to switch to the leading candidate. When the bandwagon effect finally does take hold after the next-to-last ballot, our calculations suggest that there is nothing mysterious about its presence: by the time of final balloting, a delegate interested in partaking of the spoils that accrue to the winning candidate and his supporters in the convention would be foolish not to associate himself with the overwhelming odds favoring the leading candidate. This observation, however, should be qualified by the fact that uncommitted members typically do not vote atomistically but rather in concert with some of their fellow uncommitteds — and the larger the number that acts together, the more the nonleading candidate will be favored.[49]

We are led to ask the same question asked by the authors of *The Politics of National Party Conventions* in analyzing the balloting in the 1952 Democratic and Republican conventions: "Why did they [the delegates of Kefauver, Russell, Taft, Warren, and Barkley] stay after the probability of defeat had become all too apparent?" [50] Before probing what the individual motivations of these delegates might have been, the authors offer the following general explanation: "Most of these die-hards were evidently more interested in defending a cause to which they had become attached than in finding a place on the winning side. They had assimilated a set of dogmas and had acquired the characteristics of the 'true believer.' " [51]

While our models offer no insights into the psychological motivations of the delegates, we would put forth the alternative hypotheses that their observed "irrationality" might be as much a function of:

1. their inability quickly to calculate (even implicitly) the probabilities and pivot proportions of our models — and from them to make a cool-headed and rational judgment of whom to support [52] — or,

---

[49] See Steven J. Brams, "Three Equilibrium Models of Coalition Formation in Voting Bodies", in Julius Margolis and Henry Tevne (eds.), *Theories of Collective Behavior*, forthcoming; and Steven J. Brams and G. William Sensiba, "The Win/Share Principle in National Party Conventions," in Donald R. Matthews (ed.), *Democracy and Presidential Selection* (Washington, D.C.: Brookings Institution, forthcoming 1972).

[50] Paul T. David, Ralph M. Goldman, and Richard C. Bain, *The Politics of National Party Conventions*, rev. ed. (New York: Vintage Books, 1964), p. 259. This, and the quotation that follows, are given in somewhat embellished form on p. 379 of the original uncondensed Brookings study, cited in note 6 and now out of print.

[51] *Ibid.*

[52] For amusing evidence on this point at the preballot stage, see Aaron Wildavsky, " 'What Can I Do?': Ohio Delegates View the Democratic Convention," in Paul Tillet (ed.), *Inside Politics: The National Conventions, 1960* (Dobbs Ferry, N.Y.: Oceana Publications, 1962), pp. 112–31.

2. when calculations are made, the existence of an underdog effect produced by a downturn in payoffs offered to the uncommitted members by the leading candidate (which may precede, coincide with, or follow take-off, depending on the model chosen),

as of strong emotional commitments to particular candidates. Suggestive of still other explanations is the work of Michael E. Fisher, in a branch of combinatorial mathematics known as percolation theory, on the spread of bonds that link the points of a lattice with a particular probability—and through which information might be transmitted—and that might be used to study the dissemination of information, and its effect on coalition formation processes, in a voting body.[53] As Nelson Polsby has indicated, "How news travels in conventions may determine the direction and force of stampedes."[54]

It is important to emphasize that the thresholds that we found for the four nominations above in which take-offs occurred were empirically established.[55] They were not consequences of the theoretical models;

[53] Fisher's ingenious calculation of "critical probabilities," above which clusters of infinite size spread through a lattice, seems particularly related to what take-off produces when a bandwagon for a candidate develops. See Michael E. Fisher and John W. Essam, "Some Cluster Size and Percolation Problems," *Journal of Mathematical Physics*, II (July–August, 1961), 609–19; Michael E. Fisher, "Critical Probabilities for Cluster Size and Percolation Problems," *ibid.*, 620–27; and for a review of some of the literature, Michael E. Fisher, "Cluster Size and Percolation Theory," *Proceedings of the IBM Scientific Computing Symposium on Combinatorial Problems* (Yorktown Heights, N.Y.: Thomas J. Watson Research Center, 1964). See also S. A. Roach, *The Theory of Random Clumping* (London: Methuen, 1968), chap. 5. Utilizing the mathematics of percolation theory might be viewed as an attempt to explain in more detail how a system functions by referring back to more "fundamental" processes. An example of this serial process of explanation from the natural sciences is instructive: "The biologist explains transmission of heredity in terms of DNA replication; the biochemist explains the replication in terms of the formation of complementary nucleotide base pairs; the chemist explains base pairing in terms of hydrogen bonding; the molecular physicist explains hydrogen bonds in terms of intermolecular functions; the quantum mechanician explains potential functions in terms of the wave equation" (D. F. Bradley, "Multilevel Systems and Biology," in R. G. Jones and G. Brandt (eds.), *Unity and Diversity in Systems* [New York: George Braziller, 1969].)

Cf. Holt and Turner's concept of *generative explanation* in which the analyst "must demonstrate in his explanation how the behavior in question is generated." See Robert T. Holt and John E. Turner, "The Methodology of Comparative Research," in their *The Methodology of Comparative Research* (New York: Free Press, 1970), p. 3. For further discussion of this point, see note 57.

[54] Polsby, *op. cit.*, p. 618. For an extended discussion of the effect of information in conventions—and the uncertainty produced by the lack of it—see Polsby and Wildavsky, "Uncertainty and Decision-Making at the National Conventions," *op. cit.*, esp. pp. 378–89.

[55] For Democratic conventions prior to 1936, where the decision rule was two-thirds, we found no comparable regularities distinguishing the second-to-last from the next-to-last ballots in looking at the probabilities that the first-place candidate

rather, the models provided a way of looking at the data in terms of a set of concepts whose dynamic we could study and which we could define operationally (e.g., take-off occurs on the next-to-last ballot) for the purpose of establishing empirically based thresholds that might prove useful in making future predictions. Although the theoretical predictions for take-off were generally not supported by the data, these disconfirmed predictions served the heuristic purpose of suggesting ways in which the assumptions of the models were inadequate and what competitive hypotheses need further empirical investigation in order to refine these assumptions and to develop more satisfactory models. The confrontation of the models with data, therefore, has at once (1) enabled us to determine empirically the extent to which members of a voting body act rationally and (2) forced us to ask under what conditions rational calculations might be impeded.[56]

Summary and Conclusion

Because we have summarized our calculations for the different models throughout the paper, we shall not undertake an extensive review of them here. It is less important, moreover, that we retrace the detailed calculations of our models (or Coleman's) than try to highlight the most important concepts and time-related consequences that follow from their assumptions.

For all models we assumed that two opposing protocoalitions could not combine with each other and instead could win only by gaining the support of the uncommitted members. For the pivot models, using both combinations and permutations, this assumption allowed us to calculate the proportion of pivots of each of the protocoalitions and of the uncommitted members, as well as the *cost of conflict* to the protocoalitions and the *cost of commitment* for an uncommitted member who joins a protocoalition. At the *take-off point*, this latter cost becomes a gain for the uncommitted member.

Before, coincident with, or after take-off (depending on the model chosen), this gain may begin to decrease in value at the *downturn point*

---

would obtain a sufficient number of votes (two-thirds) to win and the probabilities that the second-place candidate would obtain a sufficient number of votes (one-third plus one) to block the leading candidate.

[56] For further empirical applications of the models to the voting behavior of delegates in multiballot presidential and vice-presidential nominations using the expected-share-of-spoils concept, see Brams and Sensiba, "The Win/Share Principle in National Party Conventions," *op. cit.*

as the larger protocoalition approaches minimal winning size. We suggested that the 42 per cent threshold beyond which no candidate in a national party convention with majority rule ever progressed and then lost might be the approximate downturn point at which the payoff to an uncommitted member for joining begins to decline. While this decline may be instrumental in creating an underdog effect for another candidate, it has not so far been a counterforce sufficient to overturn the bandwagon effect for the leading candidate who has passed this threshold.[57]

For the probabilistic models, take-off occurred at the point at which the probability that the larger protocoalition became (minimal or any) winning exceeded the expected probability that a randomly selected uncommitted member would be in a (minimal or any) winning coalition. In addition to calculating the incremental probabilities that an uncom-

[57] This threshold was broken, however, in the balloting by the French Parliament in Dec., 1953, for the second president of the Fourth Republic, where one candidate (Joseph Laniel) reached the 48 per cent mark on the eighth ballot before eventually withdrawing on the eleventh ballot. (The election was won on the thirteenth ballot by René Coty.) Laniel's support began to crumble on the ninth ballot with the entry of Pierre Montel, as a new candidate, who appeared to have no chance of winning but was successful in attracting votes away from Laniel, thus creating an underdog effect for himself. See Constantin Melnik and Nathan Leites, *The House without Windows: France Selects a President* (Evanston, Ill.: Row, Peterson, 1958). Whereas a simple inductive generalization about a previously inviolate threshold is always subject to potential disconfirmation by the next case, our models suggest that low thresholds are characterized by a bandwagon (take-off) effect overriding an underdog (downturn) effect and high thresholds by the opposite play of forces. The models thus provide us with a general explanation that resolves the apparent contradiction between systems with low versus high thresholds—or the deviant case in one system or the other. However, while low versus high thresholds may be a function of the relative influence of the bandwagon and underdog effects, it is unclear under what conditions one effect will prevail over the other. For the need for finding such "limiting conditions" in the development of theory, see Herbert A. Simon, "On Judging the Plausibility of Theories," in B. van Rootselaar and J. F. Staal (eds.), *Logic, Methodology, and Philosophy of Sciences*, III (Amsterdam: North Holland Publishing Co., 1968), pp. 439–59. Simon also argues that a theory should explain *why* a generalization "should" fit the facts by providing "plausible" premises from which a generalization can be deduced. This involves specifying a set of mechanisms capable of producing the generalization, which in our case, for example, might relate how communication and contagion processes give rise to different effects in a voting body; here the mathematics of percolation theory might prove useful, furnishing us with not only a "deeper" explanation of the above generalization but also suggesting new predictions that go beyond the generalization. These predictions, in turn, might stimulate new empirical observations that allow the predictions to be tested. Theory building, then, is "not [a process] . . . of generating random hypotheses, then testing them. It is better described as a process of searching for the pattern in the data" (*ibid.*, p. 457). For further discussion, and references, on this point, see Steven J. Brams, "Measuring the Concentration of Power in Political Systems," *American Political Science Review*, LXII (June, 1968), 471–75; reprinted in Roderick Bell, David V. Edwards, and R. Harrison Wagner (eds.), *Political Power: A Reader in Theory and Research* (New York: Free Press, 1969), pp. 346–59.

mitted member could contribute to each protocoalition, we also suggested that an uncommitted member's *expected share of spoils* might be a factor in his decision to join either the smaller or the larger protocoalition. The *total probabilistic payoff*, which provided us with a concept of the aggregate benefit received by all members of the voting body at each lattice cell, turned out to have a constant value in the minimal winning case but to be variable in the any winning case.

The dynamic immanent in almost all the models, whether they were based on the equiprobability of combinations or permutations, was toward an unbalanced outcome. We suggested some factors that might contravene this dynamic, including a possible underdog effect produced at a downturn point and different assumptions about the division of spoils that tend to retard the take-off point.[58]

The empirical evidence from multiballot national party conventions with only two serious contenders supported the proposition that the leading candidate's probability of becoming minimal winning must be overwhelming—and the expected probability of an uncommitted member's being in a minimal winning coalition must be quite small—before the leading candidate is assured of nomination on the next ballot. In the four nominations analyzed, the probabilities that the leading candidates would win on the next-to-last ballot were invariably greater than on the second-to-last ballot, suggesting a relationship that transcends the peculiar circumstances and unique historical features of each of the very different nominations studied.

There may be other such invariant relationships that can be discovered with the further development of the models and their applications to other kinds of data.[59] We have not, for example, explored implications of assumptions that would permit members to switch from one protocoalition to another,[60] nor have we assessed the effect of different decision rules on coalition-formation processes. We have not considered voting bodies with three or more protocoalitions, whose dynamics of coalition-formation might be studied using three or higher-dimensional lattices. Neither have we tried to distinguish different categories of uncommitted members, such as those who do not vote atomistically but rather in concert with some of their fellows, or those who may

---

[58] For an attempt to find a major "limiting condition" (see note 57) on this dynamic, see Brams, "Three Equilibrium Models of Coalition Formation in Voting Bodies," *op. cit.*

[59] See Brams and Sensiba, "The Win/Share Principle in National Party Conventions," *op. cit.*

[60] On this point, see Coleman, "The Marginal Utility of a Vote Commitment," *op. cit.*, pp. 44–45; and Brams, "A Cost/Benefit Analysis of Coalition Formation in Voting Bodies," *op. cit.*

"lean" toward (i.e., have a higher probability of joining) one protocoalition or the other.

In complicating the models, however, it is important to keep in mind that even the calculation of lattices for two protocoalitions in voting bodies with more than ten members quickly becomes very tedious. We suspect that only a computerization of the arduous calculations for the different models will give one the flexibility needed to tailor the models quickly to a specific voting body and to quantify its coalition dynamics.[61] Nevertheless, we think that our very limited analysis of national party convention data demonstrates that even the primitive models developed at this stage can be usefully applied to empirical data.

Finally, we believe that the empirical data to which the models are applicable need not be limited to voting data. Longitudinal poll data, for example, might well be used to analyze the dynamics of shifting electoral protocoalitions (e.g., is there a take-off point in the formation of new political parties?). Other kinds of data reflecting the support or opposition of actors to particular policies or actions over time might similarly be used to assess bandwagon and underdog effects in other political arenas (e.g., the escalation of dissatisfaction with, and opposition to, a prolonged war). Clearly, much theoretical and empirical work remains to be done on the development and application of the models treated here. We hope that this work will begin to shed more light on the dynamic aspects of coalition-formation, bargaining, and other political processes.

---

[61] See Brams and Heilman, *op. cit.*, for computerized extensions of the models to larger voting bodies.

Three-Person Coalitions in Three-Person Games: Experimental Verification of the Theory of Games

4 William H. Riker
University of Rochester

IN AN earlier essay [1] in this series of volumes, I reported that subjects (mostly university students and a few businessmen) playing a three-person game remarkably close to the one around which Von Neumann and Morgenstern built their theory actually arrived at outcomes close to the Von Neumann-Morgenstern solution when they formed two-person coalitions.[2] Since, in the case of two-person coalitions, the predictions of the Aumann-Maschler solution [3] are quite similar, these subjects satisfied the predictions of that theory also. Since the solutions are not at all obvious and since almost all of the subjects were quite unsophisticated about the theory throughout their play, the fact that subjects did come close to the solution gives one considerable confidence that the solution concept is behaviorally valid as well as mathematically correct.

Subsequent to the publication of the just mentioned essay in this series, additional experiments have been reported on elsewhere [4] and they have overwhelmingly confirmed the validity of the theory with respect to two-person coalitions. Along with the results on two-person coalitions, we now have some results on three-person coalitions. These latter results also confirm the Von Neumann-Morgenstern theory, so we

The work reported in this essay was supported by a grant from the National Science Foundation.

[1] William H. Riker, "Experimental Verification of Two Theories about *n*-Person Games," in Joseph Bernd (ed.), *Mathematical Applications in Political Science, III* (Charlottesville: University Press of Virginia, 1968).

[2] John von Neumann and Oskar Morgenstern, *The Theory of Games and Economic Behavior*, 2d ed. (Princeton, N.J.: Princeton University Press, 1947).

[3] Robert J. Aumann and Michael Maschler, "The Bargaining Set for Cooperative Games," in M. Dresher, L. S. Shapley, and A. W. Tucker (eds.), *Advances in Game Theory*, Annals of Mathematical Studies, no. 52 (Princeton, N.J.: Princeton University Press, 1964).

[4] See William H. Riker, "Bargaining in a Three-Person Game" *American Political Science Review*, LXI (Sept. 1967), 642–56, and William H. Riker and William James Zavoina, "Rational Behavior in Politics: Evidence from a Three-Person Game," *American Political Science Review*, LXIV (1970), 48–60.

consequently have even stronger reason to be confident of the behavioral validity of the mathematical theorem.

This essay is a report on five cases of three-person coalitions. While the number of cases is small, the outcomes are all within the prediction of the theory, and as revealed in the protocols, subjects arrived at them by processes embodying precisely those features of coalition formation emphasized by the theory. What makes the evidence from these five cases so interesting is not, therefore, simply their rarity—although genuine three-person coalitions in three-person games have been difficult to produce in the laboratory—but rather that they confirm the theory in an entirely new direction. One could confirm the theory easily and many times over—as indeed we have [5]—with respect to two-person coalitions; but there is a point of diminishing returns. The fact that the theory is also a valid chart, even for a few instances, in an hitherto untraveled sea, strengthens our confidence in its overall validity.

The Game and the Solution

The laboratory game has the following rules:

1. There are three players, 1, 2, and 3.[6] In the five cases discussed here they were male juniors and seniors at the University of Rochester.
2. The players negotiate by pairs (1, 2), (1, 3), (2, 3), for at most five minutes per conversation, in a sequence of six to nine conversations. While a pair is negotiating, the third player is "in storage" in another room. Of course, the negotiations mainly concern how the members of a pair might divide up its potential revenue if they formed a coalition.
3. After negotiations, the players vote individually and privately on the formation of a coalition and a division of the payoff. Thus each player, i, reports to the experimenter that he (player i) has formed a coalition with player j at such and such a division.
4. If two persons agree, that is, if i says he has formed with j and j says he has formed with i and if they agree on the division, the experimenter then pays to i and j according to their agreement, provided that the amounts for i and j sum to

[5] See Riker, "Bargaining in a Three-Person Game," and Riker and Zavoina, "Rational Behavior in Politics."

[6] Detail on the subjects used as players is contained in Riker, "Experimental Verification," Riker, "Bargaining in a Three-Person Game," and Riker and Zavoina, "Rational Behavior in Politics."

$4.00 for (1, 2),
$5.00 for (1, 3),
$6.00 for (2, 3).

If two persons do not agree, that is, if only single-member coalitions form (as might happen if i votes for j, j votes for k, and k votes for i), the experimenter pays the coalitions nothing. Furthermore, the single-member coalition formed as a complement to (1, 2) or (1, 3) or (2, 3) is paid nothing. Finally, the experimenter pays nothing if the players vote for a three-member coalition with a division of the payoff among three persons.

To say, as in rule 4, that the coalition (1, 2, 3) is paid nothing is not to say, however, that it is worthless or that it cannot exist. Two smaller coalitions, e.g., (1, 2) and (3), can form (1, 2, 3) and in this case it is worth at least as much as the most valuable of the two smaller coalitions, which is $6.00 for (2, 3). The rules do not prohibit the formation of (1, 2, 3); they merely prohibit payment to a coalition that calls itself by that name. The reason for this curious distinction is that it permits the game in the laboratory to have something of the flavor of a genuine three-person game without a core as it would appear in nature. Without the restriction on payment to (1, 2, 3), subjects will, with great frequency, form three-person coalitions dividing the maximum two-person payment in three equal parts. In effect, then, they are playing a four-person game with the experimenter and are forming a three-person coalition to divide up the stakes he has offered. Since the intent in these experiments is to study three-person, not four-person, games, it is necessary to impose a rule against the kind of three-person coalitions characteristically found in symmetric four-person games. Only thus can one be certain that something like a three-person game will be played in the laboratory.

One can express these rules and the payoff schedule as a *characteristic function* or a security level for coalitions—what the several coalitions can unilaterally guarantee for themselves, provided they form. Signifying the value, v, of a coalition, (i, j), as $v(i, j)$, this function is:

$$v(0) = v(1) = v(2) = v(3) = 0;$$
$$v(1, 2) = \$4.00; v(1, 3) = \$5.00; v(2, 3) = v(1, 2, 3) = \$6.00.$$

It is understood that these values are minimal and that a coalition can in some cases make more. Thus by appropriate maneuver and negotiation, (1, 2) might actually obtain, not $4.00, but $4.50.

While the characteristic function states minimal values for coalitions, players are, of course, interested more in what they themselves get than in what the coalition they belong to gets. They get nothing without belonging to a coalition, and so they must initially be interested in the coalition payoff, but ultimately it is only the individual, not the coalition, that benefits in a real sense. The question is, therefore: "How might the values of the coalitions be divided among the members?" This is the question that solution theory is intended to answer. It is an attempt to find some equilibrium divisions of the payoff, i.e., some divisions that, from the point of view of all or a decisive subset of players, are a priori preferable to others.

As a preface to a statement of the solution of the game reported upon, I offer a brief outline of some of the main features of the Von Neumann-Morgenstern theory of solutions:

The statement $x = (x_1, x_2, \ldots, x_n)$ of the amount, x_i, that each individual player, $i = 1, 2, \ldots, n$, gets out of a game, given a set of non-overlapping and exhaustive coalitions, is called an *imputation* when it satisfies the criteria:

Individual rationality: $x_i \geq v(\{i\})$, where $v(\{i\})$ is the value of a coalition of a single player by himself. This is the requirement that a single player not accept a payment worse than he can guarantee to himself all by himself. For the game here described, this means that, since each player can guarantee himself at least zero, no one will accept a negative payment.

Group rationality: $\sum_{i \in I_n} x_i = v(I_n)$, where $v(I_n)$ signifies the value of a coalition of the whole. This is the requirement that the players altogether get what the game is worth. It is an extension of individual rationality in the sense that the players are assumed to be capable of getting what there is to be gotten. In nonconstant sum games, like the one described here, it is assumed there is an imaginary player who absorbs the unallocated amounts (e.g., when coalitions of (1, 2) form, $2.00 is unallocated and absorbed by the imaginary player).

Solutions are stated in terms of imputations: What imputations can be expected to satisfy a group of players? To express solutions, we need first the notion of *domination*, a relation expressing the social "superiority" of one imputation over another. The idea is that one imputation is *for certain* socially better than another, with respect to some coalition, if every member of the coalition makes more in the superior imputation. Formally, one says that an imputation x dominates an imputation y, with respect to a coalition S, when

1. S is not empty;
2. S is effective for x, which is to say $\sum_{i \in S} x_i \leq v(S)$, or simply that

there is enough value in S to pay off all the amounts attributed to the members of S in the imputation x; and

3. $x_i > y_i$, for all i in S.

Utilizing this notation, we can express the notion of a solution in terms of dominating imputations. A solution is a set, V, of imputations such that:

1. Every y not in V is dominated by some x in V; and
2. No y in V is dominated by an x in V.

Thus V is the set of imputations not dominating each other but together dominating all imputations outside of V. The rationale of the solution is straightforward: clearly, all the imputations not in V will be rejected by players because there is a better one in V for some coalition S. But one can not narrow the prospects further because no imputation in V dominates any other. Thus, once arrived at, any imputation in V is as good as any other for some member of some S. Practically, one may interpret a solution as the prediction that only outcomes in V occur in nature.

For the game here discussed, the solution is the following principal imputations:

	x_1	x_2	x_3	*unallocated*
where (1, 2) forms A =	1.50	2.50	0	2.00
where (1, 3) forms B =	1.50	0	3.50	1.00
where (2, 3) forms C =	0	2.50	3.50	0

and two sub-sets, V′ and V″, of imputations such that

$$\text{for V}', \sum_{i \in S} x_i = 5.00$$

and

$$1.50 \leq x_1 \leq 2.50,$$
$$0 \leq x_2 \leq 1.00,$$
$$3.50 \leq x_3 \leq 4.50, \text{ and}$$

$$\text{for V}'', \sum_{i \in S} x_i = 6.00$$

and

$$1.50 \leq x_1 \leq 3.50,$$
$$2.50 \leq x_2 \leq 4.50,$$
$$0 \leq x_3 \leq 2.00.$$

The imputations in V′ and V″, not dominating each other, together dominate all the imputations not dominated by the principal imputations.

This complex solution may be displayed geometrically. The set of all

possible imputations may be displayed in an equilateral triangle where
each side represents the worst that a particular player can do, here zero,
and the opposite vertex represents the most that a player can get, here
6.00. Every point in this triangle is an imputation because it provides
that: (1) no player gets less than his minimum and (2) the sum for all
players is the value of the game. In Figure 4.1 are set forth the possible

Figure 4.1.   Imputations in a three-person game

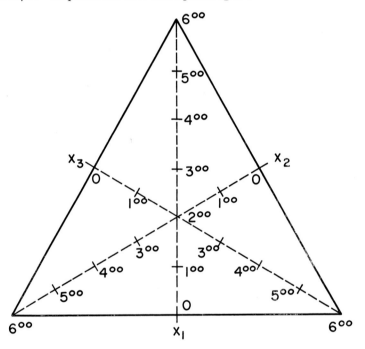

imputations for the game in question. Some sample points are: the upper
vertex is (6.00, 0, 0); the intersection of the three bisectors along which
payments to a player are measured is (2.00, 2.00, 2.00).

To depict domination, we can compare a pair of imputations by im-
posing through one point, x, axes parallel to the sides of the triangle of
of imputations, as in Figure 4.2. Moving perpendicularly from each axis
changes the payment to that player positively or negatively as indicated
in Figure 4.2. Thus, in sextant A, $x_1 < y_1$ because, with respect to the axis
for player 1, y is on the positive side. However $x_2 > y_2$, because with respect to the axis for player 2, y is on the negative side. Comparing x and
y *in toto*, it is apparent that

$$x_1 < y_1, \; x_2 > y_2, \; x_3 > y_3$$

so that, with respect to the coalition $(2, 3)$, x dominates y. In sextant B, however,

$$x_1 < y'_1, \; x_2 > y'_2, \; x_3 < y'_3$$

so that, with respect to coalition $(1, 3)$, y' dominates x. Finally, when y is on one of the axes of x, as, in Figure 4.2, y'' shares an axis with x,

$$x_1 = y''_2, \; x_2 < y''_2, \; x_3 > y''_3;$$

so x does not dominate y'' and y'' does not dominate x. (Recall, for domination to occur $x_i > y_i$, not merely $x_i = y_i$.) In general, with respect

Figure 4.2. Domination in a pair of imputations

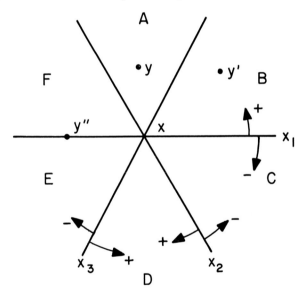

to axes through x, the imputation x dominates any imputation in sextants A, C, and E, and x is in turn dominated by any imputation in sextants B, D, and F, while no relation of domination exists between any pair of imputations having an axis in common.

Turning to Figure 4.3, it is easy to see how the principal imputations form part of the solution. Since the pairs (AB), (AC), and (BC) all have an axis in common, they cannot dominate each other. Together they dominate all the shaded areas. From $C = (0, 2.50, 3.50)$, the area shaded horizontally is dominated because it is in sextant A, with respect to point C. To interpret the other shaded areas, recall that imputation B is constructed with respect to coalition (1, 3) and leaves 1.00 unallocated (which in Figure 4.3 is attributed to player 3, but which should be thought of as going to an imaginary player). So long as it is understood that player 2 gets zero, then B dominates the vertically shaded area: for any y in that area, the point $x = B$ dominates y because $x_1 > y_1$ and $x_3 > y_3$. Similarly, imputation A dominates the diagonally shaded area with respect to the coalition (1, 2).

Figure 4.3.   Principal imputations and solution in a three-person game

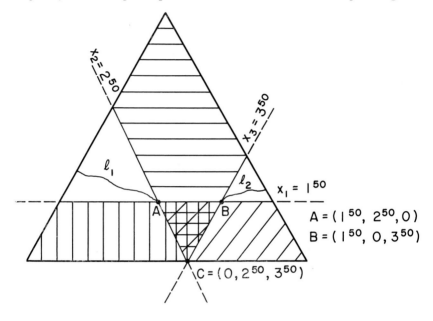

The unshaded areas can be dominated by all the points on a line running through from A and B to the nearest side, that is lines l_1 and l_2. If all the points on l_1 and l_2 (including A and B) are considered, then the unshaded area above them is dominated because it is in the several sextants A, while the area beneath them is dominated because it is in the several sextants C and E. So long as the lines l_1 and l_2 do not turn by more than 30°, no space will be left undominated. Furthermore, with respect to the coalition (1, 2, 3) no point on either line dominates any other point on the same line. (E.g., some point, $A' = (1.51, 2.51, 1.98)$, to the northwest of A, does not dominate A because, while $x'_1 > x_1$ and $x'_2 > x_2$, still $x'_3 < x_3$.). Hence l_1 is V'' and l_2 is V'.

The solution to the game reported on here is, in Figure 4.3, the points A, B, and C, and the lines l_1 and l_2. Since l_1 and l_2 are arbitrary lines, however, any appropriately restricted lines through the unshaded spaces may be part of the solution. In that sense, every point in the unshaded spaces in Figure 4.3 is an eligible imputation for the solution.

An Illustrative Match

As indicated elsewhere,[7] this game is structured so that most of the time two-person coalitions are formed in the laboratory. Furthermore, the imputations actually arrived at are apparently random variations around the principal imputations, A, B, and C. Define the quota for a player, i, as the amount allocated to i in those imputations when that amount is a positive number, that is, \$1.50 for 1, \$2.50 for 2, \$3.50 for 3. It turns out that the average payoff to i, over all matches in which coalitions (i, j) and (i, k) are formed, is remarkably close to the quota for i. This persistent approach to the quota, despite frequent slight variations, in well over two hundred matches, indicates that imputations A, B, and C may be regarded as valid predictions behaviorally as well as mathematically.

But what of the points in the unshaded areas of Figure 4.3? Do they have any role in the game? Prior to observing actual outcomes in the unshaded areas, I assumed that the lines l_1 and l_2 were irrelevant to this game because the players could not form three-person coalitions. The lines provided for a mathematical completeness but were not behaviorally significant. Much to my surprise, however, real subjects playing a game in which three-person coalitions as such were prohibited nevertheless found a way to form them. When they did so, they arrived at imputations in the unshaded areas. Since these outcomes were unexpected, they were for me convincing evidence that the fundamental notions of the Von Neumann-Morgenstern solution make sense behaviorally.

In one series of forty matches, the subjects five times arrived at imputations in the unshaded area of Figure 4.3. These imputations are indicated in Figure 4.4. These outcomes occurred quite naturally, once the subjects had invented a way to get them. Perhaps no better evidence exists of the reality and reasonableness of these events than the (somewhat edited and abbreviated) protocol of one of the matches, leading to imputation G in Figure 4.4. I therefore reprint the protocol with some editorial comment.

Subjects playing this game in the laboratory are, typically, previously unacquainted persons who become somewhat acquainted over the several weeks that are needed to play twenty to forty matches. Lacking ac-

---

[7] See Riker, "Bargaining in a Three-Person Game," and Riker and Zavoina, "Rational Behavior in Politics."

Figure 4.4.   Outcomes in experimental three-person games

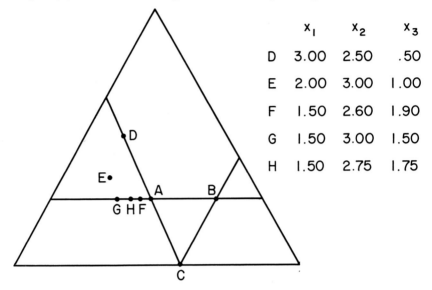

	x_1	x_2	x_3
D	3.00	2.50	.50
E	2.00	3.00	1.00
F	1.50	2.60	1.90
G	1.50	3.00	1.50
H	1.50	2.75	1.75

quaintance, they lack also the usual social methods of guaranteeing agreements (e.g., the force of law or the claims of friendship). They are thus
faced immediately with the central problem in the game, the generation
of trust. Each player is constantly engaged in trying to impress the others
with his own trustworthiness and at the same time trying to assess theirs.
In this particular series of matches, the players discovered that they
could improve trustworthiness on agreements to vote for each other by
exchanging articles of value. For example, 1 gave 2 his (1's) driver's
license (which was of value only to 1) as guarantee of his (1's) promise to
vote for 2. The understanding was that if 1 did so vote, 2 would return
the license; if not, 2 would destroy it. Of course, this agreement worked,
not because of any inherent enforcement procedure, but simply because
it made untrustworthiness riskier. Regardless of the reason such agreements worked, the subjects exploited the technique of such agreements
to develop what were in effect three-person coalitions. The following ex-
change originated with player 1, who had already developed the technique in an earlier match:

Conversation 1—Players 1 and 2

1: Do you want to start on player 3 or should I?
2: Well, what is your point?

1: I'll give you an idea. One of us sells his vote to the other and the other goes and gets player 3.

2: Meaning like, for example?

1: I mean, like, if I was going to sell my vote, you would give me a sum of money in cash and it is mine—I own it. And you have guaranteed my vote at a four dollar–no dollar split, giving you four dollars. So you have a guaranteed minimum and you can go get whatever you can out of player 3. And I would give you something like my driver's license or a blank check or something that you have every opportunity to do what you like with, if I don't vote that way.

2: That sounds pretty good. Which position would you like to have?

1: Well, you can extort a lot better than I can because you have got six dollars to play around with and I only have five dollars.

[Note that player 1 means that the maximum (1, 3) can make is $5.00, while the maximum of (2, 3) is $6.00.]

2: Yeah, so you want me to give you the money and . . . ? OK, what do I get in return?

1: As much as you can get out of player 3.

2: I mean what do I get from you to make sure you vote for me?

1: What would you like? My meal ticket, ID card, driver's license, library card, another library card.

2: Why don't you give me your wallet?

1: All right, except this [indicating an object in the wallet] is exchangeable so I will keep that.

[Note that this group of subjects are so accustomed to exchanging things of this sort that 1 does not even ask for a guarantee of return or a statement of conditions for return.]

2: OK.

1: You get the whole wallet.

2: And do you have change for a five? How much money do you want out of this by the way?

1: I think it is worth two dollars. I will let you get whatever you can out of 3.

2: Hold it, I was going to go along with it until then. Why is it worth two dollars?

1: Because you can get at least $2.50 out of player 3.

2: Yeah, well, OK. I pay you two dollars. And what kind of deal can I make with player 3?

1: Maybe a five dollar–one dollar split.

2: Why should he take that?

1: Because he can't get a deal out of me at all. All you are guaranteed security; you can't possibly lose more than two dollars because you have got my vote at four-zero if he won't cooperate.

[Apparently 1 means that 2 will get at least two dollars out of a minimum of four dollars.]

2: How about guaranteeing? Let's say, uh. I don't know whether I want to go over two dollars.

1: Well, name a number.

2: I'll say, well I would say a dollar and a half and you wouldn't agree to it.

1: I'll tell you what I'll settle for: a dollar fifty-five.

2: OK.

1: Give me a dollar fifty-five now. You have the change too. [At this point players exchanged money as indicated. Then 2 looks over the content of 1's wallet.]

2: Hope this is all yours?

1: What, you want the wallet too? And you can keep the wallet if I don't vote for a four-zero.

2: OK.

1: OK.

Conversation 2—Players 1 and 3

3: What happened in your discussion?

1: I made a deal with him that is binding. You can go chase him if you like, but you can't get my vote. I'll tell you what happened: he gave me a dollar fifty-five. I own it and I don't ever have to give it back. And by a binding technique, which is irrelevant, but it is quite binding, I am forced to vote for a four dollar–zero split. So he has my vote, but I don't have his vote.

3: You mean you are going to vote for him.

1: I guaranteed him I am voting for him.

3: Hold it, he gave you a dollar fifty-five?

1: Uh-huh. In cash. It is mine.

3: Oh. And you are going to vote for a four dollar—.

1: —zero dollar split.

3: He is getting the four dollars.

1: Uh-huh.

3: Like I would offer you a dollar and a half.

1: Can you offer me my driver's license, my ID card, my draft card, my meal ticket, anything else that was in it—I gave him my wallet, see, and I won't get it back unless I vote for four dollars.

3: I see.

1: You can go get his vote. You are not out in the cold completely. He will be forced—. The best deal he can possibly give you in order to do at all well will be like a dollar and a half or something. I don't know what he will give you

3: So.

1: It is between you and him. I am out of the game. I have got my money and I am through.

3: But you don't have your stuff.

1: The deal is: if I vote the way I said, I get my stuff back when it is all over, regardless of what happens.

3: Well?

1: See? He has got my vote guaranteed. It doesn't matter what happens to his vote. I don't care. I don't care what coalition comes out of this. I am indifferent now because I have been paid as much as I can get.

3: Oh, so you really don't care?

1: The game is between you and him. So why don't we end it [i.e., the conversation], OK?

3: Well, like if I could get your stuff back for you?

1: If you can get my stuff back—you get my wallet and I will talk to you.

3: Oh, OK.

1: I can't imagine him giving it to you. If you can do it fine, because he will be willing to negotiate with you, I think; but you just won't get very much.

3: Seems like this could come out like a three-way split.

1: Yeah, that is what is going to happen. I will get my dollar-fifty-five, and you two will split up the six dollars somehow, probably. That is my guess.

3: Well, OK, thanks for the information.

1: Well, I don't like to be mean to anybody.

Conversation 3 — Players 2 and 3

3: He told me that you had his wallet.

2: Uh-huh.

3: You gave him a dollar fifty-five?

2: Yeah.

3: So it seems to me that you would be willing to vote for me if I offered you, like, say four dollars and five cents. Is that right?

2: Four dollars and five cents and a dollar fifty-five gives me two-fifty.

[Note that player 2 means that $4.05 less $1.55 equals $2.50.]

3: Yeah. Well, you have already—you are out a dollar fifty-five and he is going to vote for you, right?

2: Yeah, right.

3: And he is going to vote for you. So, by voting for him, you will make four dollars—you will get four dollars back.

2: Yeah. But, as far as the game is concerned, if I vote for four dollars and five cents, I make two-fifty on the night—which I probably could have done without going through this nonsense.

[Player 2 here means that two-fifty is not enough because that is his quota in imputations associated with two-person coalitions. He apparently believes he deserves more than his quota for going through the troublesome negotiations to form a three-person coalition.]

3: Well, one thing I was going to ask was—like, would you like to—. Do you have his wallet in your pocket?

2: Don't touch my glasses, I remember last time.

[Player 3 had in a previous match refused to return a pair of glasses given him as a guarantee when the owner of the glasses had reneged on a promise to vote for him. Player 2 was the third player in that match.]

3: Oh, you were in the game with the glasses?

2: Yeah. I was in the game with the glasses.

3: Oh. Would you like to sell his wallet to me? For more than you paid for it?

2: Well, how much are you willing to pay me for the wallet? I never heard this one before.

3: I don't know, I never played this strategy before. I'll offer you, say, a dollar-eighty for his wallet.

2: That doesn't put me in a very good position. Then you have his wallet and I'm about to break even and then I have no deal. But, if you have his wallet, he has to vote for you, in which case —.

3: Maybe I could give you something in addition to getting his wallet; maybe I could, like, give you my wallet so that you would know that I was going to vote for you.

2: Yeah. But then you would expect to get your wallet back no matter what. I remember what happened with the glasses you know.

3: Well. No —.

2: I don't want to end up having a fight at the end of the thing. It is not worth it to me. I'd rather enjoy it [i.e., the game].

3: So would you be interested — willing to consider — like if I offer you, four dollars and ten cents, say, and gave you something of mine to prove to you that I was going to vote for you?

2: Oh yeah; then I would be willing. Then I imagine I'd make a little.

3: Yes.

2: But the whole thing is that I want to make a good deal on it and you know I don't want to be in a position where I am screwing you.

3: Yeah. I agree you should get more money for making a deal — you played the game well so far.

2: I don't know. We will see what happens. We are not going to have any time to make a definite deal.

3: We will talk again.

2: The two intermediate discussions won't mean anything much, probably, anyway.

3: Not much.

Conversation 4 — Players 1 and 2

1: How did you do?

2: Well, there was an interesting offer; but I still have your wallet.

1: [Inaudible.]

2: I wouldn't be too sure of it. There was an interesting offer made to me by 3 that he would like to buy your wallet from me. And we never settled on a price because of the time. And, well, I don't know if I am satisfied with giving you the dollar fifty-five, but I did it.

1: Well, I have got it.

2: Well, I have your wallet.

1: If you take my wallet, that is stealing, if I vote the way we agreed.

2: Well, I can sell your wallet to him before the game is over.

1: You're supposed to give the wallet back to me if I vote for you at a four-nothing split. Otherwise you are stealing.

2: I don't think so. I don't think I would be guilty of stealing it. I don't know.

1: [Inaudible.]

2: I don't know what the judicial system is.

1: Well, the value of that wallet to me is high enough that it can also amount to petty larceny; but as I think about it, it may even be grand larceny.

2: I don't know that I can steal a wallet, if I don't have it.

1: Well, you had it. I gave it to you.

2: I wouldn't have it at the time. You couldn't press charges on me. That is for sure.

1: I could subpoena the gentlemen in the room and the tape and take it to the court. My father is a lawyer and he would have a case.

2: Ok. Well, my father is a math teacher and, I don't know, I don't think he could do anything about it.

1: You would have to hire your own lawyer. That would cost money too.

2: I don't think it would get that far. All I want is the nickel back.

1: Really?

2: Yes.

1: It will make you happy if you get the nickel back?

2: Yes, it would make me happy to get the nickel back. For certain reasons.

1: I'll tell you what I will do: I'll buy back my wallet from you for a nickel when the game is over.

2: You'll buy your wallet back for a nickel when the game is over?

1: It makes me feel happier to have a dollar fifty-five in my pocket than a dollar and a half.

2: So, why not give me the nickel right now, I don't understand. Well, actually, it really doesn't make that much of a difference.

1: Or, I will vote for ah—. I can't make it a four-o-five, can I?

2: To tell you the truth I wouldn't believe the whole thing, if I didn't know that you were crazy from beforehand from other kids.

1: Let's say I would be very upset, and do things that would be unpleasant to both of us if —.

2: That is probably true.

1: If I didn't get my wallet back, that would do me in.

2: Oh, I am sure.

1: Especially my driver's license. I'm driving to Philadelphia as soon as the game is over; as soon as the game ends, the sooner I leave.

2: I am driving out to the [inaudible]. So, why don't you just give me the nickel back and we won't have anything to argue about?

1: Well, if you give me a good reason why you prefer the nickel now instead of later I will.

2: I don't know. I guess I may not trust later for something or other. Yeah, I really don't have to supply that good a reason. I just ah—it is a silly thing to quibble about but—.

1: All right I will settle for a dollar fifty. And you are safe at two-fifty.

2: That's right. I guess that is why I want the nickel.

1: [Inaudible.]

[Here 1 gives 2 a nickel.]

2: OK. So that you still have the same deal with the four-zero split?

1: Uh-huh.

2: OK. You see, I just want to be guaranteed to be officially down for at least two and a half dollars.

1: OK. I wanted to have at least a dollar fifty or so for my vote. I am willing to concede because I am not in the mood for traveling all night.

2: OK. So I guess that is about it.

1: Let's see, you understand that you are morally, legally, and otherwise obligated to return my wallet, if I vote for a four-zero split.

2: All right, certainly.

1: If somebody else gives me my wallet sooner, it would change all the agreements. If he can buy my wallet and if he buys my wallet, you are still responsible to get it back.

2: Just don't worry about it. I am bigger than the other kid anyway.

1: OK.

[This tortuous conversation may be regarded as an effort by 2 to test the feasibility of 3's offer in the previous conversation. Player 1's response in defense of his plan was intense anger that does not clearly come through in the transcript. Player 2's mild proposal for changing one dollar fifty-five to one-dollar fifty is probably a means of quieting down what might turn into an unpleasant situation. Player 1's acquiescence is probably an apology for his anger.]

Conversation 5 — Players 1 and 3

3: Do we have anything to talk about?

1: No. We're through.

3: We're through.

Conversation 6 — Players 2 and 3

3: I am planning—I have something to suggest: First of all I would buy the wallet from you for a dollar seventy-five and in addition I would give you, you know, I would give you some insurance that I am going to vote for you, ah, for a three-fifty, two-fifty split. So you would be making two-seventy total.

2: Well I don't want to sell a wallet. I'll tell you the truth I know him from— I don't know him, but he has a reputation from beforehand and when he threatens law suits I believe him for some reason or another. So, you know, I don't think I am legally liable for it, but anyway I don't want to take a chance.

3: Do you want to hold it for a while?

2: Yeah. I want to hold on to the wallet and make a deal with you so I can make some money.

3: OK. So what kind of deal do you want to make?

2: So, ah, we have six dollars to split. I like the four-fifty, one-fifty split between us.

3: Let's see, you would be getting then what? Two ninety-five to one fifty-five. OK, that sounds reasonable, I guess. Do you want me to let you hold something?

2: Well, I have to have some guarantee that you—I don't want a round robin. [By "round robin" the player meant the situation in which no pair votes for each other. Here the danger is that 1 votes for 2, 2 votes for 3, and 3 (spitefully?) votes for 1.]

3: Like, first of all, I know he is going to vote for you.

2: Uh-huh.

3: So the only thing you would want something for from me is to make sure I am not going to round robin or something.

2: That's right. Out of spite or whatever.

3: Yes, OK. Well, I don't know.

2: Do you want to hold my pencil or my driver's license?

3: OK, your driver's license would be fine. I hope no one ever asks me for my driver's license. It's in my key case.

2: If we vote for each other, you will give this back to me?

3: Oh, certainly, I don't want your driver's license.

2: OK.

3: So do we vote for—.

2: Four-fifty.

3: I get one-fifty; you get four-fifty.

2: OK.

Conversation 7; Players 1 and 2

1: I've got nothing to say.

2: I have nothing to say either.

1: Good.

2: We don't have anything to say, I think.

[In this series, the experimenter determined the time of the end of the match by a random process prior to the play. The subjects knew only that it would occur sometime in the seventh, eighth, or ninth conversation. Here the match ended at the end of the seventh conversation.]

The match ended with 2 and 3 voting for each other and the imputation (0, 4.50, 1.50), while 1 voted for 2 with the imputation (0, 4.00, 0). Since 2 had already given 1 a dollar fifty-five (revised to one-fifty), the actual imputation arrived at in the play was: (1.50, 3.00, 1.50). The course and outcome of the other four games with three-person coalitions was quite similar.

After reading the foregoing protocol, one can easily conclude that the outcome is arrived at in a most straightforward manner. It is comforting to know that this unexpected but reasonable outcome does in fact lie inside the solution of the game.